When Adulting Feels Insulting

When Adulting Feels Insulting

A Self-Help Guide for Burnt Out Millennials

Peter Guse

When Adulting Feels Insulting
A Self-Help Guide for Burnt Out Millennials

Copyright © 2025 Peter Guse
All rights reserved.
ISBN: 979-8-9922356-0-9

Published by:
Peter Guse

Table of Contents

My Why 1

Part 1: RECOGNIZE 12

Chapter 1 Recognize: How We Got Here..13

Chapter 2 Recognize: How We're Coping..25

Chapter 3 Recognize: How We Get Out..33

Chapter 4 Recognize: How Burnout Happens................................37

Chapter 5 Recognize: How Burnout Becomes a Mindset 47

Part 2: REGULATE..60

Chapter 6 Regulate: Rebooting Your System..................................61

Part 3: REPROGRAM 77

Chapter 7 Reprogram: Understanding Conditioning & Programming......78

Chapter 8 Reprogram: The Effects of Conditioning & Programming........84

Chapter 9 Reprogram: Taking Inventory of Your Beliefs 92

Chapter 10 Reprogram: Creating New Coding................................101

Chapter 11 Reprogram: Preserving Positive Programs 113

Chapter 12 Reprogram: Updating Outdated Software 125

Part 4: REDISCOVER 137

Chapter 13 Rediscover: Finding vs. Rediscovering........................138

My Why

Hi, I'm Peter, and I'm a recovering stress addict. I like to get that out of the way early, because it's a big part of why I wrote this book, and a reminder that I'm still on this healing journey today. After living much of my adult life completely burnt out, and hidden under a mask of what society and others expected of me, I'm finally getting to know myself again. Aside from that, I'm a former elementary teacher, turned corporate millennial, turned millennial self-care and mindset mentor, with over 385,000 followers on social media (still not sure how that happened, but here we are), my own podcast, and now the author of this book! So how *did* we get here, writing a self-help book for burnt out millennials?

I grew up as a typical elder millennial ('84 baby here) in northwest Indiana, where my parents, grandparents, the education system, and society in general instilled many of the same midwest/millennial values that we're all familiar with: **always work your hardest, make sure you get good grades so that you can get into a good college and get that degree that will be *the* key to your future.** Oh, and also, don't complain about your feelings— nobody likes a whiner. So, off I went into this great big world.

I was, for the most part, a straight A student, who took part in the gifted and talented programs all throughout school (*G&T kids...how are we all doing with our late or undiagnosed neurodivergence and ADHD lately?!*). I listened to my elders, competed against my peers, and took pride in all my participation trophies. I went on to college to become a teacher, because, like so many other millennials, I wanted to have purpose in my career. I wanted to make an impact and knew that becoming a lawyer or doctor was not it for me.

I graduated college in December of 2007. Yep! Right before the 2008 Great Recession. Enter the first, of many, blows to my ego. But, I was lucky enough to find a job in the exact place that I dreamed of...inner-city Chicago. No joke! I had drive and ambition like no other. I was ready to take on the challenge of inner-city teaching to make a bigger difference than just teaching in quiet, suburban Indiana. Also, I thrived on the hustle and bustle of the big city. Mr. Guse was ready to fulfill what felt like my purpose at the time. Unfortunately, that drive didn't last too long.

Enter my first encounter with burnout. This one was much more environment-driven. Don't get me wrong—I loved my students. I loved the parents and I loved my co-workers. The politics of it all got to me, though. I knew how I wanted to run my classroom to focus on more than just the test, but the charter school system I was in had different ideas. It went against everything I believed when it came to quality education, but there was a never-ending pressure to do things their way, or get fired. I'm not sure how I lasted as long as I did, but it was a near mental breakdown that led me to quitting without notice, leaving the classroom, and I never returned. As much of a relief as it was, I felt like a complete failure. For all the other educators out there, you have my whole heart!

That decision to leave the classroom ended up being the best thing I could have done at the time, because it led me to the next, much more exciting, chapter of my life. At 27 years old, I packed up whatever I could fit in my tiny Chevy Cobalt, and moved across the country by myself to California, where I started a new life. Living in California had always been on my bucket list, so just being there was enough for me. I didn't even care what I did. I worked lots of different jobs, including some really great opportunities that gave me the chance to learn more about how the brain works in both the educational space, as well as personal development. It was the confirmation that I *so* needed that sometimes, our lowest lows can launch us toward our highest highs.

In 2016, I got my dream job as a Training Specialist at Amazon Education. I nearly doubled my salary, got to travel the country presenting at school districts big and small, had a team of coworkers that made me feel like my best self at work, and started **climbing that corporate ladder**! This is where the beginnings of my stress addiction really took hold, but my motivation was high. I wore stress as my honor badge to show off my enough-ness! After not one, but two layoffs, I moved along to a much smaller company, where I grew in my career and continued to feel like I was finally "making it."

2020 had different ideas. The pandemic. Lockdowns. Inflation. The housing crisis. Looking back on it now, the pandemic and the effects of it, was the straw that broke this millennial's back. After following all the directions, and working my ass off for this long, this particular once-in-a-lifetime event is what made me seriously question if I would *ever* reap the rewards of my efforts. As much time that I'd already spent chasing the hustle, waiting for my big break to finally feel like I was getting ahead in life, the reality began to set in that I was sold a lie. I tried to hype myself up to get promoted so that I could get a pay raise, but there was a part of me that knew deep down that I didn't have the capacity to manage others, let alone myself!

But there was one silver-lining of the pandemic. Like so many other non-essential workers, I suddenly found myself with more "free time" than I'd had in years. No commutes. No social obligations. At first, I thought, *Great! I can finally catch up on everything I've been too busy for!* But instead of feeling relief, I felt... **empty.** It didn't necessarily feel like depression. More than anything, it was the realization that I had been living life just going through the motions, with no spark in me anymore. That emptiness turned into a full-blown existential crisis. Without the constant busyness to distract me, I couldn't avoid the truth anymore: *I wasn't happy.* I wasn't fulfilled. And I had no idea who I was outside of work. It was a period of my life where, for the first time, I began to challenge the subconscious beliefs, values, and truths of reality that had been running the show the past 30 years.

Over the course of the next year or so, a quiet voice just kept getting louder and louder. Not only was I completely burnt out to a crisp, but there was something telling me that I was meant for something more than just spinning on the human hamster wheel in this rat race for the next 30 years. It was like a test to see how much longer I would hold on for dear life to the system I was raised to believe was the path to success. The bottom line was, I desperately needed a break from everything, yet I also had no clear direction forward.

In January of 2022, I finally decided to take a break from my full-time position. I had no idea what I was going to do next, but I knew that I needed the space to figure that part out. I climbed down the corporate ladder and I jumped into what would become a 2+ year journey of healing from decades of built up stress that was neglected, and rediscovering a version of myself that I had completely lost touch with. While I held trust in the hope that this journey would be worth it, I was also in the most uncomfortable "in between" phase, where I had started to let go of my "old self", but yet the "new self" was still too far out of sight. Even the tiniest step outside my comfort zone was terrifying, but I knew *I* had to change for things to change.

I started by just trying to take a break and simply rest. I had these plans of starting yoga, doing more meditation, and spending more time in nature. But my brain wasn't having any of that. Every time I tried to just rest and take time for myself, there would be that narrative that went off inside my mind that said something along the lines of, "*What are you doing! Rest is lazy!*" **Sound familiar?**

If you're reading this, chances are you know the feeling. Maybe you're stuck in a job that drains the life out of you, or juggling so many responsibilities that your "free time" feels like a myth. Maybe you're so used to being busy that the idea of rest feels foreign—maybe even *wrong*. Let me guess: You've also tried the quick fixes. The trendy "self-care" routines that promise to solve burnout but feel more like adding another item to your endless to-do list. And still, here you are. ***Stuck.***

I 100% hear and see you, because I've been there…

I spent the good part of those first six months or so in a battle royale between my mind and my body. My body wanted nothing more than a nice hike in nature and a nap, but my mind continued to talk me out of it. And surprise, surprise…my mind kept winning. Even though I had saved up over a year's worth of savings, I convinced myself that I would be poor tomorrow if I didn't do something productive today. Here I was, completely burnt out and trying to take some time off, and yet burning myself out even more because my mind wouldn't shut up!

It makes total sense looking back on it now. If my worth wasn't going to be tied to my level of productivity, then what was the alternative? And the fact is, I didn't have an alternative. That was just part of the painful inner work to come. If I was going to base my worth on something else, I had to figure out what that something else was, because I was never really taught or experienced anything else.

It was a breakup from a draining and toxic relationship that convinced me to start therapy. Now mind you, I'm probably one of the most stubborn people I know. So, actually sitting down for my first appointment was a battle in and of itself. Therapy helped, no doubt, but I was still seeking more answers. Why was I like this and what's it going to take to start living a life that is true to me?! And even if I *did* figure that part out, what was it going to take to feel safe enough to take that huge leap to do things differently than I'd done my whole life? Also, therapy is expensive, and I wasn't about to pay more than I already did when I wasn't seeing the results I was expecting.

Feeling like I'd reached a dead end, I started taking things into my own hands. I went down a bit of a rabbit hole, using what I had already learned about brain science research and how our brain, mind, and body create this complex system that we call a human. I have always been fascinated by neuroscience and psychology. Instead of enjoying a nice fiction book, I've always been the type to read science articles or self-help books written by authors with a neuroscience or psychology background. I learned everything I could about burnout, from how to regulate your nervous system to how to reprogram your subconscious limiting beliefs. In the midst of all this, I also got certified as an NLP Practitioner (Neuro-Linguistic Programming), which is what led to so many of my own "aha" moments on my journey, and serves as the foundation for much of what I teach others.

Fast forward to June of 2022—I was sitting in my favorite park here in San Diego where I live, and for the first time in a **very** long time, I felt calm. I felt clear. I felt *inspired*. So what did I do? I got on TikTok! I made my first post, after having been generally invisible on social media for years. I look back on it now, and it's absolutely cringeworthy. At that time I was just trying to be a masked up imposter of what I thought people wanted to hear, but I'm so glad I did it anyways.

I started by simply sharing my journey of healing from burnout and getting back my authenticity, sharing the lows, the honest emotions, the "aha" moments, and insights. After a couple unexpected viral videos, my audience exploded to hundreds of thousands of followers. I found myself nearly overwhelmed with the amount of comments and DMs of other millennials that were so happy to hear it wasn't just them. I quickly realized I wasn't alone, and neither were they.

It seemed that my story resonated because so much of it was our **collective millennial story**. More than anything else, everyone just wanted to feel a sense of belonging where we could have these types of healing conversations out loud without the extra noise of being called entitled and whiny. What started as a way to vent turned into a mission to help others realize they weren't alone and that they *could* reclaim their lives from burnout.

Looking back now, I realize that everything I went through—from inner-city teaching, to corporate layoffs, to that third-life crisis during the pandemic—was shaping me for this exact moment. All the burnout, the breakdowns, and the breakthroughs led me to a place where I could speak with authenticity and help others navigate their own messy middles.

And while I'm honored to do my small part of creating hope and belonging for others, the community that has been built has done so much more for me than I could have ever imagined. My followers allowed me to see my true worth. They allowed me to feel good enough and safe enough to do things differently. They allowed me to break free from some of the most limiting and destructive beliefs that were dominating my life until then– that my passions were not valuable. That what I had to offer as my "gifts" wasn't good enough. That I wasn't qualified enough. They allowed me to see that these beliefs were just an illusion, based on my past. **They allowed me to see that my message was worth sharing**.

So that became my fuel. It became something bigger than myself. It became a movement of millennials that were tired of living life based on the status quo. It was a gathering space for those that were ready to do things differently. They too, came to the brutal realization that our efforts no longer produce the results we felt like we were promised, and that this entire societal structure that we've all subscribed to is nothing more than what we were taught by our parents, who were taught by their parents, and now we just consider it a truth. It was simply a repeated perception that seemed to work out pretty well for most...*until it didn't*!

Then came my next existential crisis...***what do I even call myself***?! I'm not a therapist. I have no desire to become one. Am I a mindset coach since I was trained and certified in NLP? Was I a motivational speaker? When I tried each one on for size, though, nothing really felt right or resonated. It was a conversation with a podcast guest that allowed me to see through all the usual expectations and imposter syndrome and realize what was true for me.

I'm still a teacher. I've always been a teacher. While I haven't been in a classroom in over 10 years, I was and still am a teacher at heart. It's just that now, I'm teaching ***you***, my fellow millennial burnout besties, how to understand yourself better so that you can uncover your conditioning, strip away what's no longer serving you, and build on the type of mindset that will allow you to start living ***your*** life again, and not the one you were conditioned and programmed for.

From the outside, my life isn't all that different from what it was 5 years ago. I've since returned to working full-time. I still live a humble lifestyle. I'm not out here traveling the world or doing any of the other things you oftentimes see on social media as the "F it all" dream life. On the inside, though, is where I feel the difference. I'm happier, embracing my creativity, and living a life based on my own intentions! The reward in all of this was pretty simple—**getting myself back**!

So here we are. You've picked up this book (thanks for the support!), and you're probably wondering, "*Will this really help me get unstuck?*" The answer: Yes, but only if you're willing to do the work. This book is not a magic pill or a quick fix. It's a guide to understanding why you're stuck, how you got here, and how you can navigate your way out—without losing yourself in the process. It's full of millennial culture, brain science (explained in plain English because nobody has time for Ph.D. jargon), interactive exercises, and maybe even a laugh or two. I'm not here to preach or pretend I've got it all figured out. I'm still on my own journey. But I've learned a lot along the way—lessons that helped me start building a life that actually *feels like mine*. My hope is that this book will do the same for you.

But let me be clear: This isn't about blaming society, your parents, or your employer. This is about controlling the things we actually *can* control and understanding the patterns that got you here, so you can finally start breaking them. This book is a conglomeration of everything that I've learned myself through NLP, neuroscience research, and most valuable, life experience. This is not a book where I just tell you what you want to hear. This is a **classroom**, where you are going to learn for yourself. And part of this learning community is accountability. So I'm going to push you to ask yourself the tough questions. To question what's really true and important. You're going to be prompted to get a pen out and reflect. You're going to learn new things about your brain and your mind that they never taught us in school. It might get a little uncomfortable at times, but I promise that it's all part of the process.

This is not the type of book that you read all in one sitting. It's meant to be slowly digested, with plenty of opportunities for built-in reflection and journaling prompts. While we'll cover specific strategies and techniques later in the book, the first step in this process, and maybe most difficult, is simply becoming aware of why you are the way you are, and why your brain thinks the way it does. So that's where we'll begin, and build from there.

I've organized this book into four parts, or what I like to call my **"4 R's"** framework: **Recognize, Regulate, Reprogram, and Rediscover.**

1.) Recognize
2.) Regulate
3.) Reprogram
4.) Rediscover

In **Part 1: Recognize**, we'll start with understanding just why it might be that so many millennials are feeling straight up stuck right now. We'll take a little trip inside the mind of the average millennial to better understand our upbringing, conditioning, and shared experiences. We'll dive down a mini rabbit hole of understanding the brain, mind, and body, especially as it relates to our current mindset and how our brain changes in response to stress, trauma, and constant change. One thing I've learned the hard way is that awareness *always* precedes meaningful action. You can't solve a problem when you're not fully aware of what the root of the problem is.

Then, in **Part 2: Regulate**, we'll explore what it means when we talk about nervous system regulation, with brain-based strategies to regulate your physical, mental, and emotional state. This will be less about the "what", and much more about the "why". I'm a firm believer that once you know the why behind regulation, the actual habits become ten times more powerful. None of the strategies, techniques, and reflection prompts will make much sense if we don't first lay the foundational groundwork of learning about our brains, so that we can begin to make sense of what you may be experiencing.

After you've created a heightened awareness of your conditioning, and set the groundwork for creating more internal safety for yourself, only then can you understand how to uncover and reverse the conditioning. In **Part 3: Reprogram**, you're going to learn how your mind works, like the software of a computer. I'm sharing everything I've learned from Neuro-Linguistic Programming, as well as brain science research, so that you are equipped with the knowledge to begin making powerful changes from the inside out. This is where things get really interesting, as we'll learn about how our subconscious beliefs are originally formed, solidified with experience, and how to reverse and rewire the programming that got us here to begin with.

Lastly, **Part 4: Rediscover**, is where the grand finale fireworks happen, where you'll truly begin to understand what it really means to rediscover yourself and live in alignment with who *you* are, instead of your conditioning. This is the real reward of doing the inner work. It's not about "finding" yourself, but simply uncovering the most true version of you before everyone else got their hands on you.

This is great awareness and knowledge, regardless of your generation, but I choose to focus on millennials for the simple reason that it is my own experience. Were other generations conditioned? Of course! Are other generations experiencing unprecedented levels of stress and burnout? No doubt! But it would be incredibly inauthentic of me to write about an experience that is not my own. In addition, as you'll learn, millennials are experiencing higher levels of stress and burnout than any other generation. With that said, my hope is that the concepts you'll learn in this book will be helpful, regardless of age!

Again, this is a classroom. And while much of what you'll learn is based on some pretty powerful research of the brain and mind, I also hope to pass along just as much knowledge gained from my own experiences as well. What started as taking a break to overcome chronic burnout turned into a much larger healing journey of rediscovering who I was and living for *me* again!

This is your self-help guide to **go unstuck yourself**, and I'll be your millennial mindset mentor guiding you along the journey. Before we dive in, I want you to know this: You don't have to have it all figured out to start. Healing from burnout isn't a linear process—it's messy, uncomfortable, and often two steps forward, one step back. But it's worth it. I'm not here to tell you what your journey *should* look like. Instead, my goal is to give you the tools and insights you'll need to create a life that feels like *yours*.

So, are you ready? Grab your iced coffee and avocado toast, your cozy blanket, or whatever fuels your millennial soul, and let's start peeling back the layers of stress, burnout, societal conditioning, and outdated programming. Welcome to the journey. Let's get unstuck!

This book is dedicated to the same audience and online community that has given me the confidence, courage, and words of encouragement to finally share this with you.

Part 1:

RECOGNIZE

Chapter 1

Recognize: How We Got Here

"We were handed the user manual for life only to discover it was an outdated version."

Millennials. We're known for a lot of things: our unique (and often sarcastic) sense of humor, our desire to make a difference and have a sense of purpose, our love of 90s nostalgia, and our remarkable ability to simultaneously overachieve and under-earn. Humble as we are, we'd never admit all that out loud. But there's one thing we *can* admit—and probably should—because it's the one thing nearly all of us share but rarely discuss for fear of being labeled entitled or whiny...

We're exhausted!

Not just tired—completely burnt out, extra-crispy style. This isn't just a generalized opinion. It's based on data. For example:

- Before the COVID-19 pandemic, **53%** of millennials already reported burnout. This increased to **59%** post-pandemic—higher than any other generation (Indeed, 2021).[1]

- A more recent survey found that **84%** of millennials have experienced burnout at their current job, and nearly half have left a job because of it (Rameer, 2024).[2]

- **40% of millennials** cite a lack of free time as a primary reason for burnout, while financial stress, such as paying bills and debt, ranks high across all generations but is particularly acute for millennials (Deloitte, 2023).[3]

- Heavy workloads (**50%**) and low pay (**56%**) are top stressors that disproportionately affect millennials, thanks to stagnant wages and rising living costs (Julia, 2024).[4]

- Millennials have seen stagnant or declining opportunities compared to prior generations, further fueling dissatisfaction. **Nearly 6 out of 10 (56%) of millennials are living paycheck to paycheck** (Deloitte, 2024).[5]

---

[1] Employee Burnout Report: *COVID-19's impact and 3 Strategies to Curb it.* (2021). https://www.indeed.com/lead/preventing-employee-burnout-report

[2] Rameer, V. M. (2024, January 12). *40+ statistics on burnout in the workplace you can't ignore.* Science of People. https://www.scienceofpeople.com/burnout-statistics/

[3] Deloitte Gen Z and Millennial Survey. (2023). https://www2.deloitte.com/cn/en/pages/about-deloitte/articles/genzmillennialsurvey-2023.html

[4] Julia, N. (2024, January 11). *Stress in the Workplace Statistics* (2024 Update) - CFAH. CFAH. https://cfah.org/workplace-stress-statistics/#references

[5] The Deloitte Global 2024 Gen Z and Millennial Survey. (2024). https://www.deloitte.com/global/en/issues/work/content/genz-millennialsurvey.html

Our collective exhaustion, stress, and sense of always being behind are, unfortunately, trademarks of our lives. But *why*? How did an entire generation end up entrenched in the deepest depths of a burnout pit, feeling overwhelmed and stuck in an endless loop of striving and pressure? To understand what may be causing this outside of the obvious reasons of work/life stress and late-stage capitalism that affects *everyone*, we need to go all the way back to the beginning where the seeds were first planted.

So let's start with taking a trip back in time...

When Life Was Simple

Most millennials grew up in the 90s—a decade that, in hindsight, feels almost utopian. Life was slower, quieter, and blissfully simple. It was the golden age of more carefree living. We were unplugged and unbothered. Happiness seemed to take less effort and dreams seemed more boundless. Life was slower, quieter, and, for the majority of us, less chaotic. Sure, bad things still happened, but without smartphones pinging notifications about every unprecedented event, the harsh realities of the world felt more distant.

We spent our time outside, building forts, riding bikes, and comparing our pog collections. Our biggest dilemmas were which Beanie Baby to collect next, keeping our Tamagotchis alive until recess, and deciding between *Full House* and *The Fresh Prince*—because DVR didn't exist, and VHS tapes were precious.

The internet was in its awkward teenage phase, gracing us with the screech of dial-up only when someone didn't need the phone. Smartphones? Notifications? Constant news? Nonexistent. We spent more time face-to-face instead of face-to-screen. Our concerns were confined to our hometowns, and we liked it that way.

For many of us (not all of us, of course), the 90s were the last time life felt "normal." Not only was there less things to stress about, but there was less stimulus in general, and society just operated differently. The fewer distractions gave us the space to just **be**. Bottom line... I think it's safe to say that the large majority of us miss it. We miss what life was like. It's no wonder our minds cling to that era as a mental refuge from today's relentless pace.

Nostalgia isn't just a fondness; it's a form of psychological regression—a way to reconnect with a calmer, less demanding time. And honestly, can you blame us? If the aliens offered me a one-way ticket to a planet where it's always 1998, I'd pack my Lisa Frank backpack in a heartbeat! I digress, though. Let's get back to our upbringing and how we got here.

The Playbook for Success

It's important to recognize what was happening under the surface during this time. Our (mostly) well-intentioned parents—and society at large—gave us a playbook for success. Their motivations were heartfelt: they wanted to give us opportunities they never had, prepare us for a competitive world, and ensure we had better lives than theirs. The playbook was simple: *work hard, get good grades, go to college, land a job, and success will follow.* It was a fairly straightforward path, neatly packaged with a shiny prize at the end. All we had to do was stay on the grind.

This well-meaning intention, however, translated into a high-pressure environment where achievement reigned supreme. Productivity became synonymous with worth. Rest was earned, not essential. Messages like *"If you've got time to lean, you've got time to clean"* seeped into our subconscious. Without realizing it, our young minds internalized the belief that success required constant hustle. We started equating our *value* with our *output*.

Staying busy wasn't just encouraged—it was glorified. The mainstream image of success was the overachiever who could manage school, work, sports, friendships, and some dream job, all without breaking a sweat or needing a therapist. It looked easy in the teen rom-coms, didn't it? Yet, the real message was loud and clear: success meant relentless effort, and if you weren't getting what you wanted out of life, maybe you just needed to *work a little harder*.

These narratives and belief systems, while motivating, also laid the foundation for a mindset that equated success with constant effort and achievement. While we were enjoying the last moments of calm and soaking up the simplicity of our youth, deeper lessons about productivity and success were being quietly installed deep into our subconscious. And as anyone in the *"Therapy in Your 30s Club"* can attest, those subconscious beliefs don't just disappear. They become the driving force behind our actions and emotions.

Before we knew it, we transitioned from human beings to human *doings*. Oblivious to how much the world would change, we followed the rules, adopting a belief system built for a different time. Little did we—or our parents—know just *how* drastically the world was about to flip upside down.

When the World Turned On Its Head

As we prepared to step into adulthood, the world we had trained for began to unravel before our eyes, morphing into a reality that was unpredictable and unforgiving. In 1999, the Columbine school shooting shattered the illusion that schools were safe havens. Overnight, one of our most secure spaces became a source of fear, where we no longer felt safe in the place where we spent half of our day.

Then came the dawn of the new millennium. Who could forget the buildup to the year 2000? Y2K hysteria had everyone bracing for chaos. Would all the computers shut down? Would society collapse? As we watched the clock count down on the night of December 31, 1999, the world collectively held its breath—and exhaled when nothing happened. Life went on. But in hindsight, that uneventful New Year's Eve was merely the calm before the storm.

The morning of September 11, 2001, is seared into the collective memory of our generation. At a very young and impressionable age, we watched a terror attack happen on live TV. Many of us probably remember our teachers turning on the news, somehow thinking that our developing brains would be able to make sense and process what was happening. Most of us couldn't. That day, everything changed, and our brains would never be the same. The attacks on the World Trade Center and other landmarks shattered the sense of safety that many of us had taken for granted. Suddenly, the world felt much more dangerous and unpredictable.

I remember sitting with my family that night, eating dinner on the couch and watching the news. Like so many others, I was trying to piece together what it all meant. Were we going to be okay? First, our schools couldn't keep us safe from gun violence. Now, our country couldn't stop terrorists from hijacking planes and crashing them into iconic structures? And because many of our parents were also in a state of shock and didn't know how to process what had happened with us (let alone for themselves), much of that trauma went left unchecked. It was another defining moment that marked the end of the relative peace and stability we had come to know and, perhaps, became too comfortable with during our childhoods.

These events didn't just rattle us—they rewired us. Our young, impressionable brains learned to anticipate the worst and operate in survival mode. It felt like our youth slipped away in an instant. We had to grow up fast, adapt, and brace ourselves for whatever came next.

From there, it felt like we could barely catch our breath. The 2000s were a relentless parade of challenges: economic recessions, wars, environmental crises, and rapid technological advances that reshaped the world. The carefree simplicity of childhood was quickly slipping away, replaced by anxiety about whether we could "make it" in this ever-changing world. And with all this worry and anxiety seeping in, our instincts were to revert to what we were taught: *just work harder*. So we did!

For many of us, that meant going to college. We worked tirelessly, envisioning the moment we'd walk across the stage, degree in hand, ready to conquer the world. After years of effort, the payoff seemed within reach. Finally, we'd reap the rewards of following the playbook. Unfortunately, similar to many of the other pivotal and key moments in our lives, the world had another blow to our ego in store.

Enter, the 2008 Great Recession. Just as so many of us were entering or getting ready to enter the real world, we got knocked right back down again. Overnight, the job market collapsed, housing prices plummeted, and financial institutions that had seemed too big to fail were suddenly on the brink of collapse. For many millennials, this crisis was a harsh introduction to the realities of adulthood. Jobs were scarce, and those lucky enough to find work often settled for part-time roles, low wages, or positions outside their field of study. It wasn't just about financial instability—it was about shattered trust. Trust in institutions, in the promise that hard work would lead to success, and in the traditional milestones of adulthood. Buying a home? Starting a family? Saving for retirement? All of it suddenly felt out of reach, leaving us feeling more and more disillusioned and uncertain about our future.

Somewhere in this whirlwind, we lost sight of the fact that downtime is just as valuable as overtime and that humans are only capable of handling so much at one time. But just like Chumbawamba said, *"I get knocked down, but I get up again."* So we did. We brushed ourselves off and listened to that little voice in the back of our minds that said *"just work a little harder."*

The Never-ending Rat Race

As millennials were attempting to find their footing in a shaky economy, the idea of "hustle culture" began to *really* take off around this time. The more packed our schedules were, the more valuable we felt. Just as we once chased gold stars and tried to make our parents proud with perfect report cards, we were now seeking the approval of our Baby Boomer bosses and corporate overlords. Those company-sponsored Friday happy hours became a celebration of who was the best of the stressed that week, and who accomplished more than anyone else.

Around that same time came the uprising of social media, which added a new layer of pressure. Platforms that were meant to help us connect became tools for comparison and showing off our achievements as another way to get validation. We'd scroll through carefully curated feeds and feel like everyone else was doing just a bit better than us. As if that wasn't enough, the boundary between work and life blurred with smartphones that brought emails and pings wherever we went. We could be "on" 24/7—and many of us felt like we had to be. The pressure to stay "connected" created an ever-present anxiety that only added to the stress and burnout that many millennials were already experiencing.

As the economy began to recover, it finally felt like maybe—just *maybe*—we could start to breathe. This was our time! All we had to do was climb that corporate ladder and prove our enough-ness through our level of productivity, and maybe we could actually have a piece of the pie. Perhaps our brain was finally finding evidence that hard work *does* pay off! It might have taken a solid 10 years, but some of us were *finally* able to afford a home, or pay down our student loan debt for that degree that we don't even use anymore. But, you guessed it, the world had yet another once-in-a-lifetime event that nobody saw coming.

Enter 2020– COVID and the pandemic. All of a sudden, we were forced into isolation, where we didn't have access to those that would normally be able to support us in our day-to-day lives. The trauma of watching the ticker go up every night on the news of how many people died was followed up by insane inflation, the housing crisis, massive layoffs, and an increase in unemployment rates. The list goes on. As we wrestled with these seismic shifts, it became increasingly clear that the world we were navigating was not the one we were promised. The neatly laid plans—the ones we were told would guarantee success—kept crumbling beneath us. Instead of thriving, many of us felt like we were stuck in an endless uphill climb, never quite reaching the summit. Exhausted and disillusioned, we asked the same question we'd been asking for years: *How much more can we take?*

Of course, there are always critics. "Life's hard for everyone," they scoff. "Stop being such whiny, entitled millennials." The difference, however, for millennials is two-fold. First, these challenges hit us during critical milestones—the moments we were most excited to achieve long-anticipated goals. Buying a home, starting a family, building a career—each milestone came with its own special world-shattering crisis. Second, the very beliefs we clung to—the ones about hard work leading to success—seemed to work for previous generations. Baby Boomers and Gen X worked hard and achieved the dream: the house, the retirement fund, the stability. But for us? Those same beliefs haven't served us quite as well. Instead of paving a clear path to success, they've left many of us burnt out, disillusioned, and wondering if the finish line even exists.

We were taught to believe that the blueprint for success was simple: work hard, get an education, secure a stable job, buy a house, and eventually enjoy the fruits of our labor in retirement. But what we didn't account for were the seismic shifts in the economy, job market, and society as a whole. Skyrocketing home prices, student loan debt that feels like a lifelong subscription that we're desperate to cancel, and an economy that plays hopscotch with stability turned that once-reliable dream into a distant fantasy for many of us.

Inside the Mind of a Millennial

Burnout, for millennials, is more than just the result of busy schedules or the inability to "cope." It's a reflection of systemic change and relentless stress compounded by a culture that insists on hustle over healing. We're not just burnt out—we've been conditioned into a burnout mindset. This mindset is hardwired into us as *the* thing we were taught to believe would unlock success. Instead, it's become a mental loop we can't escape, leaving us stuck between societal expectations and a reality that keeps pulling the rug out from under us.

Fast-forward to now. Here we are, collectively crispy, and battling a chronic case of **U.H.E.F.**—Unprecedented Historical Event Fatigue. It's like being thrown into survival mode over and over, without enough time to catch our breath before the next fight or flight response. Even so, we've spent years doing everything we were "supposed" to do, only to realize the goalposts keep moving.

You may feel like you are constantly falling short, unable to meet the benchmarks of success that were set for you. The belief that we should be able to achieve the same milestones, despite the vastly different circumstances, creates a sense of guilt and shame, as we internalize the idea that our struggles are a result of personal failure rather than systemic changes. **Everything just feels more and more heavy,** and at some point in time, the pressure begins to test your will to keep working harder.

This gap between expectation and reality has left many millennials feeling like they're constantly playing a game of catch-up, but the rules of the game keep changing without warning. We find ourselves wondering, *"Why am I not further along?"* or *"What am I doing wrong?"* when, in reality, the system we were trained to succeed in no longer exists in the same way. We're trying to win a race in which the finish line keeps moving—and it's exhausting. The kicker? Many of us still believe—deep down—that if we just push a little harder, we might finally achieve that long-promised satisfaction and stability. Yet, this isn't about working harder; it's about living differently. But more on that later.

Based on what we were taught and told, we anticipated that our efforts would lead to a reward. But what seemed to work out for generations before us, just doesn't seem to work anymore. Our dopamine tanks are running on empty, with little to no motivation for much of anything beyond the bare minimum, let alone work. Yet at the same time, our brain is **wired** to use the same type of programming that we were taught growing up.

We're stuck in a mental loop because it was never taught or modeled for us how to slow down. Rest? That's lazy. Downtime? Better use it to be productive and start a side hustle. We've internalized these messages so deeply that even in moments of stillness, we're haunted by that inner voice (probably wearing your parents' faces) that whispers, *"Shouldn't you be doing something?"* That constant need to prove our worth has become the very thing that is exacerbating our already chronic levels of burnout.

The result? Rest isn't restorative; it becomes a source of stress rather than a time to recharge. It becomes a reward for finishing your to-do list rather than the fuel to tackle it in the first place. And even when we do manage to step back, the world labels it as *quiet quitting*, guilting us into falling back in line. This is where *"I can't even"* becomes a daily reality.

But here's the thing: We're not lazy or entitled—we're *exhausted*. We've been sold a script that doesn't match the reality of the world we live in anymore. When effort repeatedly fails to yield reward, it's no wonder our brains and bodies start to wave the white flag. This is where many of us slide from fight-or-flight into *freeze mode* (hello, dorsal vagal shutdown). Where your body and your brain begin to dissociate from each other, like you're just a brain that's carrying around this body stuffed full of emotions, but no energy to actually process it.

No hobbies. No passions or goals. No energy to process emotions. Sound familiar? Our brain simply doesn't have the capacity for those things! If our modern lives were depicted as *Schoolhouse Rock* episodes, they would be called *"Dissociation Nation", "Self-Isolation Station",* and *"Burnout Roundabout."*

This brings us to the core of why we, as millennials, are so prone to burnout. It's not just about being tired—it's about a deep, pervasive exhaustion from constantly trying to live up to seemingly impossible standards. We've worked smarter *and* harder, yet the rewards still feel out of reach.

Our brains are wired to believe that if we just keep pushing harder, we'll get there—but where is "there?" And at what cost? *And,* can we really keep going like this for the next 30-40 years? We were taught to grind, but nobody taught us how to truly rest. And now, we're facing the consequences of a lifetime spent in hustle mode without the tools to properly recharge.

Burnout **isn't** a personal failure—it's a result of systemic changes, shifting expectations, and a world that demands more than we can give. And when you combine a shaky economic landscape, an unpredictable job market, and the constant pressure to appear like you have it all together, it's no wonder we're all feeling SO. DAMN. TIRED!

We've been wired to believe that if we just keep working hard enough, we'll finally "make it"—but when is enough, *enough*? And is it possible for you to fathom that you might just be enough, regardless of how busy and productive you are?

Take a deep breath, my friend. For now, simply recognizing how we got here is the first step to unraveling and unlearning all of this.

Chapter 2

Recognize: How We're Coping

"Tired Like I'm 80. Wired Like I'm 20."

Let me be very clear. This isn't a pity party. Yes, we can talk about how we got the short end of the stick, but we're not here to dwell on that. There's probably a bit of truth in it as well, but that will only keep us stuck living in victim mode for the rest of our lives. Instead, I'm walking us through this in great detail to highlight what we *can* change by truly understanding the roots of why we are the way we are and identifying what's actually in our locust of control. It's the awareness of some of those more deeply seated root causes, like our subconscious programing and mindset that serves as the foundation of real change.

One of the things that you'll hear me say a lot in this book is that our brain has one main, and very important job. That is to make sure that we stay alive and survive another day. *Period*. One of the most effective ways that it helps us do this is by creating coping, or protective, mechanisms to shield us from current or potential threats. These mechanisms are our brain's way of saying, "This stress is too much, and I need to feel safe." At first, they feel like shields —helping us manage the chaos—but over time, they can become walls, boxing us in and perpetuating the very stress we're trying to escape.

By unpacking these coping strategies, you might not only feel more seen and understood but also realize that your habits—those things you sometimes beat yourself up over—are really just survival tactics in disguise. And guess what? Survival tactics can also be rewired.

Common Coping Mechanisms

To keep this a bit more general, there are four main coping strategies that stand out as commonalities for many millennials, based on what we were taught, saw modeled, or experienced through our own life: **self-isolation, dissociation, regression, and hyper-productivity**. Each of these is a response to stress and pressure, but each also tends to reinforce the burnout cycle that so many of us know all too well.

Let's explore why we tend to rely on these behaviors and how they connect to our brain's need for safety, control, and comfort.

1.) Self-Isolation: Retreating for Safety

For many millennials, emotional regulation wasn't exactly a family strong suit. When we were upset or needed to let off some steam, the go-to response from our parents often sounded something like, *"Go to your room and cry it out. And shut the door while you're at it."* They weren't being cruel; they were simply modeling what they had been taught—handle your emotions privately and without disrupting others. And so, we followed suit, adopting the same coping mechanism of **self-isolation** without ever learning healthier alternatives.

Fast forward to today: When stress becomes overwhelming, many of us default to retreating inward. Locking ourselves in our rooms, avoiding social interaction, and seeking solitude often feels like the only way to regain some semblance of control in the midst of chaos. It's our brain's way of saying, *"If you don't give me space to process, I'm going to shut down entirely."* In a world where digital connectivity is at our fingertips, self-isolation has also become easier than ever. We can be *physically* alone while maintaining the illusion of connection through social media—no awkward vulnerability required.

Now, let's clear something up: taking time to yourself isn't inherently bad! Alone time can serve as a much-needed reset, a way to reconnect with yourself at a deeper level. It's the perfect opportunity to indulge in your favorite granny hobbies (crochet and gardening anyone?), or to simply unwind without external demands. The risk lies in overdoing it. The longer we self-isolate, the easier it becomes to disconnect from the very support systems that help us feel seen, heard, and healed. Worse yet, we often guilt or shame ourselves for needing that alone time in the first place, which only adds to our stress.

So, let's reframe self-isolation. It's not something to feel ashamed of—it's an invitation to get curious. What's driving your need to retreat? What patterns are showing up? Use the prompts below to reflect and explore:

- **What or who am I trying to escape from when I self-isolate? Is it a specific person, environment, or feeling?**

- **What do I get to avoid by self-isolating? Is it conflict, discomfort, or something else entirely?**

2.) Dissociation: Mentally Checking Out

When the going gets tough, the tough get going—until they hit a wall and can't go any further. That's when **dissociation** oftentimes shows up, offering a deceptively simple solution: *If I don't think about it, it's not happening, right?!*

When stress becomes too overwhelming, the brain has a nifty trick up its sleeve: it "checks out." Dissociation is essentially your brain's mute button, a defense mechanism that lets you sidestep the noise, hit pause, and numb out for a bit. This might show up as zoning out during conversations, binge-watching entire seasons on Netflix, or scrolling endlessly on your phone. These are all ways of avoiding what's bubbling under the surface—because if you're too busy doomscrolling, you don't have to deal with it.

In today's overstimulated world, needing a mental break is completely normal. So, just like self-isolation, dissociation isn't *inherently* a bad thing. It's a protective mechanism designed to shield you from emotional overload. In the short term, this mental "time-out" can be a relief, helping you avoid the weight of feelings that feel too heavy to carry. But when dissociation becomes a default setting, it can trap you in a loop of avoidance. You start to miss the bigger picture, lose touch with the good stuff (like joy!), and—here's the kicker—end up reinforcing the stress you were trying to escape in the first place.

Think of dissociation like a shaken soda bottle. Every time you avoid negative emotions and "save them for later," you're shaking the bottle a little more. Eventually, there's so much pressure that it takes enormous energy just to keep the cap on. When you finally unscrew it, it's not going to be pretty. That's why staying stuck in dissociation tends to eventually fuel the burnout cycle.

Now, this doesn't mean you need to beat yourself up for mentally checking out. We all do it—it's human. The key is to become aware of when you're dissociating and to notice when you *do* have the capacity to start processing some of those feelings. You *deserve* to feel the full spectrum of your emotions—yes, even the tough ones—so that you can truly feel the joy and relief that comes on the other side.

Let's reframe and get curious about it! Take a moment to reflect and journal on these questions:

- **What emotions might I be trying to avoid or struggling to process?**

- **What do I get out of avoiding those emotions? (Hint: We wouldn't do it if there wasn't *some* benefit.)**

- **What am I missing out on by avoiding those emotions?**

3.) Regression: Seeking Comfort in the Familiar

So, why is it that millennials have such a warm place in our hearts for 90's nostalgia? Whether it's music, fashion, toys, or those Saturday morning cartoons, nostalgia lets us reconnect with a time when things felt easier. When physical escape isn't possible, our brains are pretty crafty at finding a mental one.

Enter **regression**, a coping mechanism that pulls us back to a time when we felt safer, calmer, or more in control. With a strong desire for more safety, we may oftentimes find ourselves remembering and regressing to a time in our lives where things *did* feel more safe.

Humans are wired to seek what feels familiar, especially in uncertain or stressful times. When our current reality feels too chaotic, our brain starts scrolling its highlight reel for moments when things *were* easier. Your brain doesn't really care whether those memories are happening in real-time or are just being replayed. The same neural networks fire up, allowing you to temporarily "borrow" that sense of calm from the past—even if your present reality is a dumpster fire.

Regression is like hitting pause on adulting. It probably explains why so many of us joke that we don't feel like "real adults." Our body might be reminding us that we're getting old, but our mind is still stuck at a time in our lives when we were 20 years old. Revisiting these safe, nostalgic spaces is an entirely natural—and honestly, pretty clever—way to calm ourselves when the present feels too overwhelming.

I hope it goes without saying that it is 100% perfectly fine to revel in 90s nostalgia! It's part of who we are! Blast your favorite throwback jams, rewatch your comfort shows, and wear that *Friends* hoodie proudly. Again, it's simply an awareness (I know, I know- probably sounds like a broken record).

While revisiting the past can give us temporary relief, there's a fine line between seeking comfort and avoiding the present altogether. Spending too much time in regression mode can keep us stuck, preventing us from tackling what's right in front of us. So, by all means, use nostalgia to create a sense of peace—but then channel that calm into fuel for facing the elephant in the room.

Ready to get curious? Take a moment to reflect and journal on the following questions:

- **When was a time in your life that things felt more "normal"?**
- **What made that time feel easier or safer?**
- **What problems might you be avoiding by mentally retreating to that time?**

4. Hyper-productivity: Escaping by Doing More

We've all been there: you finally get a weekend free to relax, but instead of taking the time to rest, you somehow find yourself cleaning out the garage or reorganizing your bookshelf. Even though you're running on fumes, you talk yourself into ticking off every task that *could* wait—because who can resist a good checklist!

Unlike other coping mechanisms that involve retreat, hyper-productivity is all about diving headfirst into doing—never pausing, never resting. Staying busy becomes a way to avoid the discomfort of facing the stress under the surface. As counterintuitive as it sounds, hyper-productivity is a defense mechanism in its own right—by staying busy enough that we don't have to face our feelings.

This was 100% me! Instead of enjoying some quality self-care time when I caught a break, I would sit down for just long enough to create a new to-do list with 10 more chores that I could be doing instead. For millennials, staying busy has long been a badge of honor. We feel validated when we're busy because it makes us feel productive, as if constant movement equals progress. But the more we praise busyness, the harder it becomes to see how it contributes to our own burnout.

When we're hyper-productive all the time, we trick ourselves into feeling like we're in control. But in reality, we're only avoiding deeper issues. Keeping ourselves busy provides the *illusion* of productivity, but it's often a way to avoid confronting the emotions and stress we'd rather not face. If we're constantly achieving, we don't have *time* to confront the uncomfortable truths bubbling beneath the surface. Over time, though, hyper-productivity can leave us exhausted, and the stress we've been avoiding will still be there, waiting for someone to address it.

What's even more fascinating (and honestly a bit terrifying) is how our brains can become **addicted to stress**. Yep, addicted. Just like we can crave sugar or caffeine, our brains can get hooked on the "high" of productivity and busyness. In essence, we are subconsciously addicted to the very thing that we're trying to consciously create less of...***stress!*** This constant state of alertness, or "fight or flight," becomes a kind of comfort zone. But here's the thing: our bodies aren't built to function in constant stress. Eventually, something's going to give—and it's usually our mental and physical health.

Now, stress itself isn't inherently bad. It's the thing that pushes us to finish projects, meet deadlines, and accomplish goals. The problem arises when we rely on *staying* stressed in order to avoid dealing with the stress we've already ignored. The key is awareness: recognizing when our productivity is masking deeper emotional issues.

Take a moment to reflect and journal on the following questions to better understand any patterns of hyper-productivity in your own life:

- **What emotions does staying busy allow you to avoid?**

- **How might your constant need to do more be contributing to your burnout?**

- **What's one thing on your to-do list that can wait for tomorrow so you can prioritize taking care of yourself today?**

Whatever coping habits you identify with—whether it's retreating, zoning out, escaping into nostalgia, or drowning yourself in tasks—they're not signs of failure or weakness. They're just responses that we learned along the way that are now wired into our brains as habits to help us survive. They're all driven by a desire for safety, control, and relief, and when our stress response is triggered, our nervous system reacts in ways that prioritize short-term survival over long-term healing. They each have their place, but they can also hold us back if we're stuck in autopilot.

These are the "masks" and "shields" that we put up to not only avoid the uncomfortable, but to avoid being seen for our most vulnerable selves. We plaster on a smile and say *"It's fine. I'm fine. Everything's fine"*, when, in fact, we are *not* fine.

By recognizing these habits with curiosity instead of judgment, we give ourselves a chance to decide what changes we actually want to make. Again, these coping mechanisms are not inherently "bad". In fact, they have helped us navigate difficult periods in our lives. The problem arises when they become our default responses, preventing us from truly addressing our underlying burnout. By understanding why we turn to these behaviors, we can begin to shift away from them with compassion and awareness.

Chapter 3

Recognize: How We Get Out

"Sometimes you have to break down everything you thought you were to become who you were always meant to be."

As millennials, the beliefs we hold about rest, productivity, and busyness didn't just appear—they were ingrained through our upbringing, education, media, and societal narratives. These beliefs, while they've helped us achieve certain things, have also kept us trapped in cycles of burnout and stress.

We watched previous generations find stability through sheer hard work. For them, this approach worked. But for us? It's a different world. The one-size-fits-all playbook no longer fits, and it often feels broken. But we have nothing to replace it, so we convince ourselves that pushing ourselves beyond our limits is the only way forward. Over time, our brains become hardwired for this mode—so much so that it becomes our default. Stress, exhaustion, and burnout become part of our identity. In a strange way, stress becomes part of our comfort zone. Even though you might not *think* it feels too comfortable, this pattern of thought and operating mode is and has been running the show for most of our lives.

Now, don't get me wrong: I'm not suggesting we all quit our jobs and live on a beach (though, let's be real, that sounds pretty nice). We still have bills to pay, and the world isn't going to wait for us to feel ready. What I'm saying is that we've been conditioned to believe that hard work is *the* key to success and happiness, but this version of success is quickly becoming obsolete. The world we prepared for no longer exists. The linear path of education, career, and stability that our parents followed has been disrupted by economic instability, technological advances, and shifting social norms. But, we keep trying to follow it. We cling to this belief that if we just push harder and hustle longer, we can still get ahead.

This disconnect between our conditioning and the reality of the world today leads to a form of cognitive dissonance. There's a sort of unconscious bias toward what we've observed that worked for others, and yet it's not working for us. We're applying outdated solutions to modern problems, which leaves us frustrated and overwhelmed, wondering why the strategies we were taught aren't yielding the success we were promised. We wonder how we're ever going to keep going like this and look forward to the day we can finally retire and enjoy our lives, but that seems to be a bit of a farfetched pipe dream by now.

Which brings us to the big, uncomfortable question: **why wait?** Why wait until retirement to experience peace and calm? If the old ways of doing things aren't working, then what *will*? And how can we find balance between ambition and well-being?

I absolutely *dread* the phrase "work smarter, not harder." It's another corporate colloquialism, and it doesn't address the root issue. Perhaps it's not about working smarter—maybe it's about working within the constraints of today's reality, rather than clinging to what we've been taught.

To change the game, we need to acknowledge the origins of the rules that some group of guys made up a couple hundred years ago, and start to challenge those deeply ingrained subconscious beliefs that are no longer working in our favor. Our worth *doesn't* need to be tied to our productivity. Recognizing that is the first step in creating a healthier relationship with both rest and work.

So, where do we go from here? How do we break the cycle of burnout and reclaim our sense of self-worth, especially when the world we live in feels more and more stressful? The first step is understanding that this isn't entirely our fault, *but we are the only ones who can take responsibility for changing it.* We've been taught that rest is a luxury and busyness is a virtue, but it's time to challenge those outdated beliefs. Redefining these beliefs means seeing rest not as a luxury, but as a vital aspect of our overall well-being, and embracing it without guilt is essential for us to be able to fathom something better.

The rules have changed, and so must our approach to life. We can no longer measure our success by the standards of past generations. We need to define success on our own terms—whether that means taking a break, setting boundaries, or simply allowing ourselves to exist without always having to be "doing" something. We can't create more hours in the day, but we *can* create the internal conditions that allow us to fully embrace rest when the opportunity arises.

Even when we recognize that these beliefs are no longer serving us, changing them isn't easy. Societal pressure, fear of the unknown, and the discomfort of breaking away from the norm keep us stuck in these outdated ways of thinking. But, if your brain is in a default mode of fight or flight right now (which, let's face it, is likely the case), this is the worst possible time to try to figure out the solution. When we're stressed, our brains aren't equipped for creative thinking or problem-solving. So don't stress out about how to fix this in the moment—we'll circle back to this once we understand how to shift out of that default state.

For now, think of it like this. You are in your **chrysalis era**. You've spent your entire life chugging along like that delicate caterpillar that always feels like it's falling behind, but it keeps going anyways. Now, it's time to retreat into a cocoon of self-reflection and growth, shedding the old programming that no longer serves you.

Here, you'll learn to simply rest as you allow your mind to deconstruct everything you've always known and begin to reconstruct for the butterfly you were always meant to be. This isn't a time to rush things. Just like a chrysalis, if you cut it open before it's divine timing, you ruin it. And, don't forget this other important fact about the chrysalis—it has to stay away from toxins. They will only delay the process even more. So, cut out the toxicity.

This isn't just about overcoming burnout. This is about overcoming the conditioning and programming that creates the pressure and urgency that leads to burnout in the first place. It's about discovering the power of your creative mind when your survival mind finally relaxes. It's about having passions and goals again that got buried by a need to simply get through the day. And it's about getting your spark and "wings" back so that you can start living life on your own accord, instead of everyone else's!

In this cocoon, allow yourself grace and compassion. This is your chance to reparent your mind, to teach your brain there's a new way of living and being. The wings are coming—but you have to be okay with where you are now. Yes, look forward to that day where you spread your wings and fly. Keep that mental movie in the back of your mind as the stable and consistent source of internal motivation to keep going. But also allow yourself to be ok if you're not there yet. There's some inner work that needs to be done first. Remember, the breakdown always comes before the breakthrough (cue *"Butterfly"* by Crazy Town).

Now that you're starting to create more internal awareness of how we got here and where we are today, it's time to go down the rabbit hole of the brain and mind science of burnout. Buckle in, because you're about to learn just how burnout happens and how it becomes so ingrained that it becomes a whole-ass **mindset**.

Chapter 4

Recognize: How Burnout Happens

"Stress is like throwing a rock in a pond. There's the rock splash, and then the ripple effects. One is more in our control than the other."

If there's one thing to know about your brain, it's this: **its number one job is to keep you alive and safe**. Not successful, not blissfully happy, not Zen—just alive. Your brain has one job, and it takes it very seriously.

We've already covered the societal pressures and conditioning that have paved the way to burnout. That's the straightforward part (though not exactly the cheerful one). The trickier piece of this burnout puzzle lies in the neuroscience—the dynamic relationship between your brain, body, and mind under stress.

The good news? Your brain is not set in stone. You'll hear me compare your brain to a living, breathing computer quite a bit throughout this book, so let's set the stage:
- **The hardware** is the physical structure of your brain. Think of it as the circuits, chips, and components that make the whole system work.

- **The software** is how your brain is wired based on repeated patterns of thought, belief, and behavior. This is the programming that determines what the hardware does.

This relationship is dynamic. The software sends instructions to the hardware, which then responds and shapes the software further. It's a constant feedback loop between the brain and the mind, where the mind creates the brain, which creates the mind and vice versa. So, to address the problem, we need to focus on both optimizing the hardware (brain), and updating the software (mind).

Unlike a regular computer, however, your brain is constantly adapting, always influenced by the inputs it receives. This adaptability is called **neuroplasticity**—the brain's ability to rewire over time. And for us millennials, that's a game-changer. It means that, while we may be conditioned to repeat certain patterns, we're not doomed to stay stuck in them. We can move beyond survival mode, and break free from the stress-addicted loops of burnout we've been running on autopilot. Where we are now doesn't have to be where we are forever. But before we start talking about solutions, we need to understand how burnout happens in the first place. You can't debug the system if you don't know where the glitches are, right? This chapter will help you pinpoint the glitches and make sense of the hardware and the software.

Stress: The Double-Edged Sword

Let's start with this: *stress isn't inherently bad*. In fact, it's what keeps us functioning. Stress is the thing that gets you out of bed in the morning—well, that and the fear of being late after hitting snooze seven times. Cortisol, our favorite stress hormone, is usually at its highest in the morning, although this may not be the case if your cortisol levels are dysregulated (Clow et al., 2004).[1] That surge of cortisol when you first wake up is like a little nudge, saying, *"Hey, we've got stuff to do—let's not die today."*

But when you're in burnout mode, that pep talk is more like an endless, high-alert siren right in your face. Instead of motivating you to tackle the day, it keeps you in a state of hyper-vigilance, wearing you down before you even get started. To understand how this all goes haywire, we need to unpack the brain's stress response. Because if you want to debug the burnout program, you need to understand the code.

When you encounter stress, it's as if your brain's computer kicks into overdrive. Alarms go off, resources are redirected, and all systems focus on managing the perceived threat. This isn't a glitch; it's a built-in program. Your brain is wired to prioritize your survival over everything else.

The key player in this program is your **autonomic nervous system (ANS)**. It has two operating modes:

- **Parasympathetic nervous system (PNS):** Also known as "rest-and-digest" mode, this is where your body repairs itself, digests lunch, and generally keeps you feeling safe and functional.

- **Sympathetic nervous system (SNS):** The infamous "fight-or-flight" mode. This system is activated whenever you're stressed, anxious, or threatened, and unfortunately, burnout keeps many of us stuck here on a loop.

---

[1] Clow, A., Thorn, L., Evans, P., & Hucklebridge, F. (2004). The awakening cortisol response: Methodological issues and significance. *Stress*, 7(1), 29–37.

Your SNS acts like a sophisticated security system, springing into action at the first sign of danger. Two key players in this system work together to keep you alive:

- **The Amygdala**
  This tiny, almond-shaped structure in the brain's emotional center is like the alarm system. It processes emotions and stores highly emotional memories. While it handles both positive and negative emotions, it's hardwired to react faster to negative ones (Guex et al., 2020).[2] Think of the acronym **FAST**. When the amygdala detects something scary, it hits the panic button. FAST.

- **The Hypothalamus**
  Once the amygdala sends out its SOS, the hypothalamus takes over. It's like the control center for your body's autopilot. The hypothalamus kicks the **autonomic nervous system** into gear, taking charge of involuntary functions like heartbeat and breathing. It also activates the **hypothalamus-pituitary-adrenal (HPA) axis**, which releases stress hormones like adrenaline and cortisol into your system.

---

[2] Guex, R., Méndez-Bértolo, C., Moratti, S., Strange, B. A., Spinelli, L., Murray, R. J., Sander, D., Seeck, M., Vuilleumier, P., & Domínguez-Borràs, J. (2020). Temporal dynamics of amygdala response to emotion- and action-relevance. *Scientific Reports, 10*(1). https://doi.org/10.1038/s41598-020-67862-1

This dynamic duo is like your brain's version of pushing the "turbo boost" button. Suddenly, your heart starts pounding, your muscles tense up, and you're ready to either confront the threat or run away from it as fast as you can. Whether you like it or not, this is your body's built-in system to both wake you up and wear you down.

So how does all this tie back to burnout? When your SNS is constantly activated—thanks to never-ending emails, deadlines, worldly events, and doom-scrolling—your brain and body never get a chance to switch back to the PNS. This is the glitch in the system we'll unpack throughout this chapter.

The Human Evolution of Stress

We all know what stress *feels* like, but let's simplify what it *is*: **stress is your brain's natural response to unexpected change**. Let's keep it as simple as possible, right?! Anytime reality takes an unanticipated turn, your brain flips into high-alert mode—because if it didn't, you wouldn't be here reading this book.

For our hunter-gatherer ancestors, this reaction was life-saving. Imagine you're strolling the savannah, hunting dinner for your family, when you hear a rustle in the bushes nearby. It could be a harmless bunny. Or a sabertooth tiger ready to pounce. Without concrete evidence either way, your brain defaults to assuming the *worst-case scenario*. Why? Because keeping you alive is its number-one priority, and it would rather be safe than sorry.

This preparation for the worst-case scenario happens incredibly quickly, bypassing the need for much conscious thought. Your **amygdala**—that trusty alarm bell—instantly activates your **stress response**, flooding your body with adrenaline and cortisol. This surge helps redirect resources away from nonessential functions and toward survival mechanisms (like running for your life). Your **prefrontal cortex**—the part of your brain responsible for logic and planning—takes a back seat as all available energy is redirected toward immediate survival (Arnsten, 2009).[3]

This "drop everything and survive" programming might explain why you get brain fog or can't focus during stressful situations. Your brain isn't interested in solving complex problems or thinking about long-term planning when there's even just a chance of being metaphorically eaten.

If the rustle turns out to be a bunny, no harm done. But if it's a tiger? You're already primed to fight or flee. This default reaction is deeply ingrained in our biology on purpose.

This **negativity bias**—the tendency to focus on potential threats over positive experiences—was key to our ancestors' survival. Your brain will *always* prioritize "sticks" over "carrots". Our ancestors who worried more about sticks lived another day to gather more carrots. Today, however, it just means we're all stuck in worst-case-scenario mode most of the time. Our brains are more and more like glue for the bad, and oil for the good. No wonder pessimism feels so natural sometimes. It's not you; it's your brain doing exactly what it's designed to do.

Now, I know you're dying to know what's in the rustling bushes. Lucky for you, it was just a rabbit. Once your brain realized there was no real threat, your stress response started to dissipate, typically within about 90 seconds. You returned to a state of calm, or homeostasis, and survived to live another day. But if it *had* been a tiger, not only would you have been ready to react, but your brain would also store the memory of that danger. The rustle, the fear, the fight-or-flight response—it all gets locked into your brain's library of "things to worry about later." So the next time you hear a similar rustle, your brain is even more prepared to sound the alarm.

---

[3] Arnsten, A. F. T. (2009). Stress signalling pathways that impair prefrontal cortex structure and function. *Nature Reviews Neuroscience, 10*(6), 410–422. https://doi.org/10.1038/nrn2648

Now luckily, we don't have to worry as much about tigers in the bushes today. In modern life, stressors are less about physical survival and more about emotional and social pressures—work meetings, deadlines, and social media notifications. The thing is, your brain can't distinguish physical from psychological threats (LeDoux, 2012).[4] So whether it's a rustle in the bushes, a passive-aggressive email from your boss, or an uncomfortable conversation with a loved one, it sounds the same alarm.

This is why **perception** plays such a big role in stress. It's rarely the event itself that triggers your stress response; it's how your brain *interprets* the event. For example, if you've ever been blindsided by a last-minute work meeting that turned into a layoff announcement, your brain remembers that emotional trauma. So the next time a surprise meeting pops up on your calendar, your amygdala freaks out before you've even clicked "join."

This pattern is your brain's way of trying to protect you. Once the threat is gone, your system is supposed to return to normal, like a computer cooling down after a spike in activity. But here's the problem: unlike physical stressors, emotional and social stressors don't have a clear endpoint. Your brain can tell when a tiger runs away, but it struggles to recognize when an email or a period of financial hardship is no longer a threat. And the more frequently your stress response is triggered, the more your brain *expects* it.

It's like your brain is constantly scanning for sabertooth tigers, even when all that's really there is a harmless bunny. Over time, this constant anticipation wears you down, keeping you stuck in a cycle of stress and burnout.

The Ripple Effects: When Stress Becomes the Norm

This is where stress goes from a single "rock splash" to an endless series of ripples, affecting everything in its path. A shaky economy spirals into worst-case-scenario thoughts of another recession. A last-minute meeting invite

---

[4] LeDoux, J. (2012). Rethinking the emotional brain. *Neuron, 73*(4), 653–676. https://doi.org/10.1016/j.neuron.2012.02.004

triggers fears of being fired or laid off. Your brain stays busy ruminating on all of the possible worst case scenarios until it's able to confirm or deny whether one or none of those predictions are true.

If you're constantly stressed, by either repeated rock splashes or ongoing ripple effects, your body never gets a chance to fully recover, which can lead to a range of physical and mental health problems. Cortisol plays a crucial role in this process. When you're stressed, your body releases cortisol to help you cope with the situation. In small doses, cortisol is beneficial—it helps you stay focused and alert. But when stress is constant and those rock splashes turn into repeating ripples, your body gets flooded with cortisol and adrenaline. If your brain is a computer, then this is the equivalent of overheating.

Think of acute stress as a quick sprint—a burst of energy and focus to handle an immediate challenge. Tight deadlines, sudden arguments, or unexpected problems activate this system, giving you the boost needed to survive the moment before returning to calm. Now, imagine running a marathon, not just once, but every single day, without rest or water breaks. That's what happens when acute stress turns chronic. Your brain becomes overworked, fatigued, and, eventually, it malfunctions.

Over time, this repeated activation of the stress response begins to shift your brain's baseline. Instead of returning to calm, it stays on high alert, always prepared for the next potential threat. Your brain is adaptive, and repeated stress can actually change its wiring, reinforcing stress responses. Imagine a path through the woods—the more you walk it, the clearer it becomes. Unfortunately, this well-worn path becomes your brain's new "normal."

This neuroplasticity is a double-edged sword. On one hand, it allows your brain to become more efficient at responding to stress. On the other hand, it can also make stress your brain's new normal. Unfortunately, this means that over time, your brain becomes more likely to default to a stress response, even in situations that don't warrant it. Essentially, you're stuck in survival mode, where the hardware (your brain) is continuing to operate on the same software (your mind).

If we take a moment for some more 90s nostalgia, you could think of this like *Windows 95*—constantly glitching and freezing under the weight of your stress until you close out some of your 57 open tabs. It's not that your brain can't function. It's just that it's not optimized to handle all of these modern day stressors and the associated thoughts all at once.

This is burnout in action. It's not just the "rock splashes" of new stressors that wear you down—it's the ripple effects amplified by past experiences, conditioning, and the unresolved stressors your brain keeps replaying.

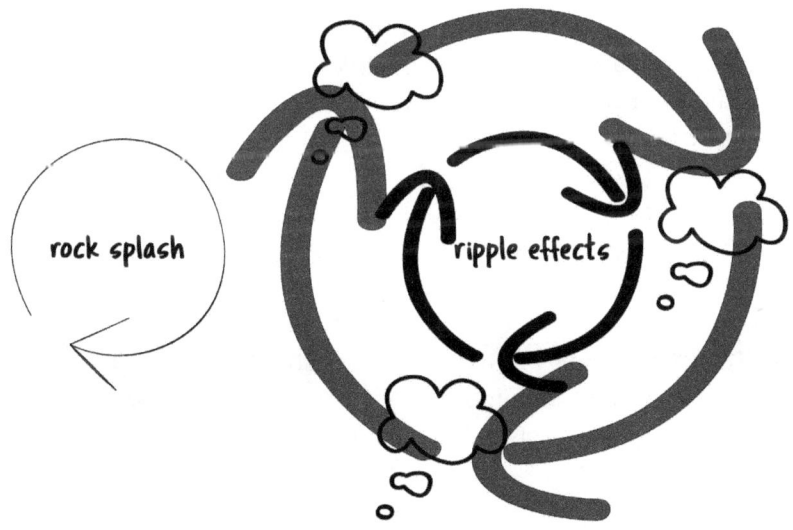

In burnout, your brain and body stop working in harmony. The brain stays stuck in survival mode, convinced it's not safe to relax, while the body is utterly drained. It's a constant battle, where your body begs for rest, but your mind insists you keep pushing because the perceived threats haven't disappeared. It's in this cycle where your stress response goes on repeat through thought alone.

Initially, burnout might feel like a temporary state—something that happens after a particularly tough week or month. You tell yourself, "*I just need to get through this, and then I can relax.*" But as the stressors continue and you don't find time to recover, burnout starts to feel less like a passing phase and more like a permanent condition. This shift happens gradually. You might start to believe that feeling exhausted, overwhelmed, and disconnected is just your new normal. You begin to identify with these feelings, and they start to influence how you see yourself and your place in the world. Instead of recognizing burnout as a response to specific circumstances, you start to view it as an inherent part of your identity.

This ongoing state of stress starts to wear down your brain's ability to function properly. The more your stress response is activated, the harder it becomes for your brain to switch off. Eventually, it overheats, slows down, and may even crash. Burnout can, by all means, happen due to the "rock splashes" alone, but it's those "ripple effects" that are reinforced by both your conditioning and your previous experiences that keep so many of us stuck there.

Just like when you hear that rustle in the bushes, and your brain reminds you of that one time from your past when this happened, each time you encounter a situation that triggers your conditioned stress response or reminds you of a past stressful event, the neural pathways associated with stress become stronger. The more your brain defaults to stress, the more likely it is to continue doing so, and the more likely those rock splashes will become stronger, and the ripple effects will last longer.

The tough and unfortunate truth, however, is that stress isn't just going to go away. It's a necessary part of life to keep us safe and alive. But stress isn't something that's supposed to consume your life. While we may not be able to control the rock splashes of everyday stress, there are certainly things that we can do to make sure the rock splashes don't become lasting ripple effects.

By now, it should be making a bit more sense why we're all so on edge. The early 2000's brought a wave of one unprecedented historical event after another and, not only has that wave just continued into our everyday adult lives, but it has become so frequent and we have such easy access to this triggering information, that our brain has become entrained to expect it. This is where things start to go from burnout to a **burnout mindset**.

Chapter 5

Recognize: How Burnout Becomes a Mindset

"You can't think your way out of burnout when you're already hardwired for it."

Before diving into how burnout takes root as a mindset, let's revisit a few critical concepts:

1. **Your brain's #1 job is survival.**
   Its primary function is to keep you alive and safe, even if that means prioritizing short-term protection over long-term well-being.

2. **The amygdala: Your brain's alarm system.**
   This tiny but mighty structure reacts to external threats by referencing associations to past experiences. If something reminds you of a previous

stressor, your amygdala can trigger the same stress response—even if the current situation isn't actually threatening.

3. **Memory shapes stress responses.**
   Your memories are like a stress highlight reel. When you recall a stressful event, or experience something related to a previous stressful event, your brain reactivates the emotional and physiological responses tied to that memory, preparing you to face similar situations again.

4. **Stress sidelines your logical brain.**
   Under high stress, your brain shifts energy to the sympathetic nervous system—also known as the fight-or-flight response. This means your logical brain (hello, prefrontal cortex) gets put on hold, making it harder to think clearly, solve problems, or plan ahead.

In essence, your brain is a master of recycling stress. Encounter something that even vaguely resembles a past stressful event, and it's like hitting play on an old mixtape—your brain reacts to the present event in the same way you've reacted to associated memories.

This is where burnout starts to control your life. When your brain keeps replaying these stress responses without a reset, the software begins to control the hardware more and more. The result? Burnout shifts from being an occasional state of overwhelm to a chronic mindset—one that influences how you see the world, handle challenges, and even view yourself.

The Hardware and Software of Your Brain

Let's go back to our trusty computer metaphor to help make sense of this. The hardware of your brain is its physical structure—neurons, synapses, and neural networks. It's the foundation that allows you to think, act, and experience the world. But the magic truly happens in the software—your mind. This is where the deeper processing occurs, governing your automatic thoughts, feelings, and behaviors

Your subconscious mind operates as the brain's **operating system**, running quietly in the background. This is where deeply held beliefs, experiences, and conditioning live. It's the invisible program shaping how you perceive and react to the world. And because of that, you're probably unaware of most of what's running in the background.

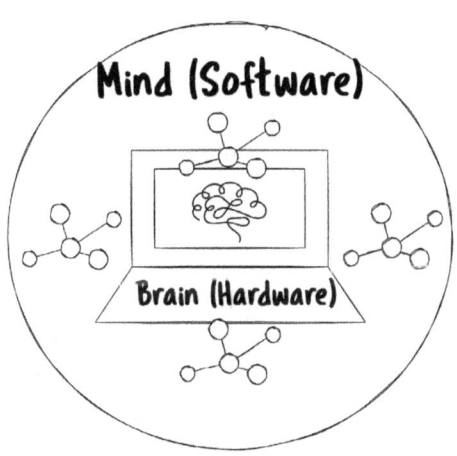

It's why watching *Jaws* makes us fearful of going in the water. Most of us have probably never been attacked by a shark. But watch that movie, and suddenly open water feels ominous. Your brain, master of making emotional associations, has now linked the ocean to shark attacks—even if it's irrational. That's the power of subconscious programming.

This is why two people can face the same situation and have totally different responses. One person might see a challenging work project as an exciting opportunity, while the other sees it as an overwhelming burden. It's not the task itself that's different; it's the **brain's interpretation of the task**, shaped by past experiences and beliefs, that determines whether the stress response is activated (Harvey et al., 2010).[1]

---

[1] Harvey, A., Nathens, A. B., Bandiera, G., & LeBlanc, V. R. (2010). Threat and challenge: cognitive appraisal and stress responses in simulated trauma resuscitations. *Medical Education, 44*(6), 587–594. https://doi.org/10.1111/j.1365-2923.2010.03634.x

Picture yourself on a roller coaster. You're inching up the first massive hill, heart racing, palms sweating, breath quickening. Now, are you thrilled—or terrified? Physically, your body reacts the same way. But how you *label* the experience depends on your brain's associations and perceptions. If past experiences link roller coasters with fun, you'll likely feel exhilarated. If they associate roller coasters with fear, you'll want to bolt for the exit. That's how powerful memory is in dictating our stress response.

This is because your brain has been wired to associate certain cues—like a tone of voice, a type of situation, or even a particular time of day—with stress. These associations are stored in your brain as "shortcuts" to quickly activate the stress response and protect you from danger. It's efficient, but not always accurate.

It's a bit like training a dog to sit when it hears a command—over time, the dog learns to associate the sound with the action. Similarly, your brain learns to associate certain situations, thoughts, or emotions with a stress response. When your brain perceives something as stressful, it searches your memory for similar past experiences. Then, based on what it finds, your brain triggers the same emotional and physical response you had the last time something like this happened. Essentially, you're not just reacting to the present; you're **reliving past experiences as though they're happening right now.**

In many cases, this backfires. Your brain might react to a minor annoyance—like a colleague correcting your work—as if it's a catastrophic failure. That's because the shortcut your brain took skipped nuance and jumped straight to "threat detected." In other words, your brain's *perception* of threats is highly influenced by your past experiences and conditioning.

For example, if you grew up in an environment where mistakes were harshly punished, you might be more prone to perceiving errors as catastrophic, triggering your stress response more easily. Similarly, if your brain is used to a stable and consistent stream of negative events and trauma, such as the timeline of events that we discussed in Chapter 1, you'll be more prone to expect the next bad thing around the corner before it even becomes part of your reality.

In other words, you begin to stress about stress before stress happens. This may eventually get to the point where even when life is relatively calm, it feels unnatural—like something is missing. So your brain goes hunting for the next bad thing, priming itself for chaos that hasn't even happened yet.

This leads to a default mode, creating a mental pattern where calm feels uncomfortable, and stress feels normal. I like to call this FOMOA.

Fear Of Missing Out on Anxiety

Fear of Missing Out on Anxiety...

It's when your brain starts panicking because it's been a whole hour, and nothing bad has happened. A five-alarm mental fire ensues, scrambling to find a crisis to maintain its "normal" state! This pattern isn't logical—it's algorithmic. Your subconscious software is programmed to expect stress and chaos, so it seeks and creates more of the same. By recognizing this algorithm, you can begin to find ways to interrupt it.

The Algorithm: The Brain's Filtering System

Much like how social media platforms curate your feed based on what you've previously interacted with, your brain filters through the endless stream of sensory information bombarding you every day to determine what's most important. And when I say endless, I mean *endless*. Research suggests your brain is hit with around **11 million bits of data every second**—sounds, sights, smells, and more. The thing is, your conscious brain, the hardware, can only process **less than 100 bits of data per second** (Markowsky, 2024).[2] That's like trying to watch a fireworks display through a pinhole.

To determine what gets filtered in, your brain prioritizes stimuli that align with what you believe, expect, or other unconscious biases (Purves et al., 2018).[3] If you're convinced that your value lies in productivity, your brain's filtering system will highlight every missed deadline, every late-night email, and every task still looming on your to-do list. It will also conveniently filter out evidence that challenges this belief—like the fact that no one's judging you for taking a lunch break. It's kind of like that one friend who only hears what they want to hear. It's selective, picky, and sometimes, a little dramatic.

When your brain flags something as "important" (say, a looming deadline that feels like the apocalypse), it sends this information to the amygdala. The amygdala then decides whether to sound the alarm based on its memory bank of past emotional experiences. In a balanced system, the amygdala's response is appropriate to the situation. But when your brain is constantly filtering for stressors, your amygdala can become hyperactive, triggering the stress response more frequently and intensely than necessary.

Everyday stressors—like a busy workday, a disagreement with a friend, or a looming deadline—are a normal part of life. However, when these stressors are filtered through the lens of your conditioning and subconscious beliefs, they can be amplified, making them feel much more overwhelming than they actually are. It's why that text message, phone call, or worst of all, the knock at the door, triggers you beyond belief. Not only is it an added stimulus that you

---

[2] Markowsky, G. (2024, November 22). *Information theory | Definition, History, Examples, & Facts*. Encyclopedia Britannica. https://www.britannica.com/science/information-theory/Physiology

[3] Purves, D., Augustine, G. J., Fitzpatrick, D., Hall, W. C., LaMantia, A.-S., & White, L. E. (2018). *Neuroscience* (6th ed.). Oxford University Press.

simply can't handle right now, but those are the very things that trigger our very sensitive built-in alarm in our brain.

This interaction between the filtering system, amygdala, and previous memories creates a powerful feedback loop. The brain filters input based on what it deems is most important to you now. Then, that filtered data gets put together like a puzzle and your brain creates an internal interpretation, which is highly influenced by your subconscious beliefs. Your response, especially when you're stressed, is driven by patterns from your past, therefore reinforcing this same cycle in your brain's wiring. It's a **self-perpetuating cycle** that can make burnout feel inescapable. As they say, "where the focus goes, energy flows."

The cycle goes something like this:

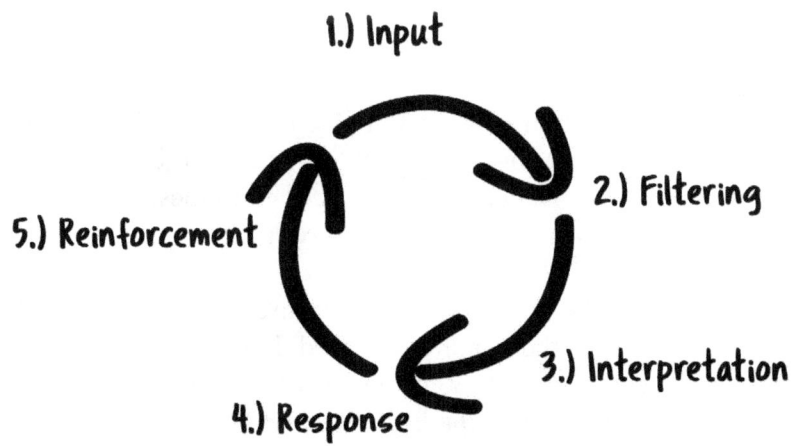

1. **Input**: You encounter a situation—a project at work, a social interaction, or even just your morning routine.
2. **Filtering**: Your brain quickly scans the situation based on your subconscious programming, values, and where your attention has been

directed. If your programming is stress-focused, your filtering system will highlight anything that could be perceived as a threat or challenge.
3. **Interpretation**: The filtered information is sent to the parts of the brain that make meaning and the amygdala, which interprets it as either safe or dangerous, based on associations to previous experiences (even those that you may not consciously remember). If the amygdala senses danger, it triggers the stress response (and access to your logical, thinking brain decreases).
4. **Response**: Your body reacts to the stress signal, increasing your heart rate, tensing your muscles, and releasing cortisol. You may feel anxious, irritable, or exhausted as a result. Your response, in this moment, is going to be highly based on patterns of your past rather than conscious, logical thought.
5. **Reinforcement**: The stress response reinforces your subconscious programming, making your brain more likely to filter for stressors in the future. Your reality becomes increasingly filtered through a lens of stress and burnout.

Eventually, this cycle distorts your perception of reality. You start to see the world as more and more stressful and threatening (even when it might not be, at least to the extent that your subconscious makes you believe), causing you to put off rest and rebalance. As the cycle continues to repeat, burnout becomes more than just a state—it becomes your default mindset.

While those breaks where there's no present threat would normally be a time to take a breather in the marathon called life, they instead become an opportunity to prepare ourselves for whatever next worst case scenario our anxiety-ridden brains are anticipating. It's those *"what ifs"*, produced by our own minds, that keep us stuck in a very unproductive busy mode. Over time, this feedback cycle creates a sense of hopelessness and cynicism, where you start to believe that no matter what you do, you'll never escape the cycle of stress and burnout.

From Burnout to Burnout Mindset

When burnout becomes more than just a short-term experience—when it turns into a **mindset**—it reshapes your expectations about yourself, your capabilities, and your future. It infiltrates every aspect of life—work, relationships, and even your sense of self-worth. Suddenly, exhaustion feels inevitable, work becomes synonymous with overwhelm, and life itself seems like an uphill battle. These embedded expectations influence your decisions and actions, shaping your reality in ways that keep you stuck in the cycle.

Your internal dialogue plays a significant role in this process. When you're burnt out, it's easy to fall into negative self-talk: *"I'm not good enough to be successful,"* *"I can't handle this,"* or *"I'll never catch up."* Negative self-talk is like a **virus** in your brain's software—it corrupts your programming, distorts your perception of reality, and reinforces the stress and burnout cycle between your filtering system and amygdala. Suddenly, the world around you seems to confirm your worst fears—stressors feel bigger, challenges more unsurmountable.

Negative self-talk not only affects your perception but also primes your amygdala to be more reactive. When you constantly bombard yourself with negative thoughts, your brain interprets this as a sign that you're in a threatening environment. The amygdala, always on the lookout for danger, becomes hyper-vigilant, triggering the stress response more easily and frequently. The brain's neuroplasticity means that these stress-related patterns can become ingrained, making it feel like burnout is an inescapable part of life.

This mindset becomes a **self-fulfilling prophecy.** The more you believe you're stuck, the more stuck you become. Challenges start to feel impossible, and even small wins feel insignificant. You begin to see the world through a lens of hopelessness, convincing yourself there's no point in trying.

This cycle of confirmation is powerful. Each time you encounter a stressful situation, your burnout mindset kicks in, telling you, *"See? This is just how life is."* You then respond to the situation with the usual protective mechanisms that allow us to prolong dealing with it in ways that reinforce your burnout—by dissociating, self-isolating, pushing yourself too hard, or neglecting self-care. These behaviors only reinforce the cycle, confirming your expectations and making burnout feel more entrenched. It's a **loop**: your thoughts fuel your actions, your actions reinforce your beliefs, and the pattern repeats.

It's like being trapped in a never-ending replay of the same stress-filled day. Societal conditioning and neuroplasticity work together here, deepening the grooves of this mental record. The beliefs we inherit—about productivity, worth, and busyness—combine with the brain's wiring to create patterns that feel impossible to break.

Here's the good news: the same principles of **neuroplasticity** that lock in these burnout patterns also offer a way out. By creating new, healthier habits and beliefs, you can rewire your brain to reduce stress and cultivate a more balanced mindset in a world where stress is simply not going away!

But let's be clear—this isn't about slapping a bandage of "positive thinking" over years of burnout. If your subconscious programming screams, *"You're not enough,"* repeating *"I am enough"* ten times a day won't suddenly convince your brain. Positive thoughts alone won't cut it; they need to align with your deeper beliefs and subconscious wiring.

This goes back to one of the important concepts to remember about your brain on stress: **you can't think your way out of burnout.**

Why "Thinking" Your Way Out of Burnout Doesn't Work

In a healthy brain, the **prefrontal cortex**—responsible for reasoning, decision-making, and self-control—acts as a counterweight to the **amygdala**, the brain's alarm system. The prefrontal cortex evaluates whether a perceived threat is real and whether a stress response is appropriate. But chronic stress flips the script. The amygdala grows stronger and more dominant, while the influence of the prefrontal cortex weakens.

This shift makes sense in life-or-death scenarios, where split-second reactions matter more than careful deliberation. But in everyday life, it means your brain defaults to emotional reactions and subconscious programming, rather than intentional choices and logical thinking. This is why you can't simply "think" your way out of burnout—because in this state, **your forward-thinking brain is offline**, causing you to live your life based on past conditioning vs. free will.

When your stress response activates, your brain doesn't weigh options or assess new strategies. Instead, it digs into its archives for past patterns and emotional associations. It filters in those 50 or so bits of data out of the 11 million, and then your mind does its thing to fill in whatever is still missing. This efficiency model—using stored experiences to guide reactions—can become problematic when those past experiences are packed with unprocessed emotions and negativity. And when you've got a mind full of negative emotional experiences from your past, many of which have never been fully processed, that gives the emotional reaction brain a lot of opportunities to base our reactions off of which might not be all that logical.

Even when you *know*, consciously, that this old way of doing things is destructive, you can't seem to help yourself but to "just keep swimming" and reacting in the same ways you always have because that's part of your subconscious programming and has become a hardwired habit. This belief system is so deeply ingrained in our subconscious that we don't even realize it's driving our actions. We've learned to associate busyness with value, and as a result, we've become subconsciously hyper-focused on staying stressed.

Escaping this mindset requires more than willpower. It demands:

- **Conscious effort** to reprogram your subconscious beliefs.
- **Retraining** your brain's algorithm to interpret stress differently.
- **Calming your amygdala** to reduce the intensity of your stress response.

By challenging your beliefs, practicing positive self-talk, reparenting yourself, and gradually exposing yourself to new experiences, you can start to shift how your brain filters and responds to information.

This doesn't mean eliminating stress—stress is inevitable. Instead, it's about rewiring your brain's **default reaction** so stress no longer dominates your life. It's about creating a space where you can rest without guilt, shame, or distraction.

The first step is **awareness**—recognizing when you're operating in a burnout mindset. Pay attention to your thoughts, how they influence your emotions, and how those emotions drive your behaviors. Notice when your stress response is triggered and ask:

- **Is this reaction truly warranted? (And it might very well be. So don't try to deny it. Simply challenge it.)**

- **Am I responding to the current situation based on my current reality, or am I responding based on an association to something that happened to me in the past?**

Once you've recognized the patterns, it's time to address both the **hardware** (your brain and nervous system) and the **software** (your beliefs and programming). Just like you can upgrade your computer's operating system, you can reprogram your brain to stop defaulting to burnout. You just need to learn how to manage the inputs so your brain doesn't feel the need to keep hitting the panic button every time something unexpected happens.

Before we can even begin to do this inner work of changing the "software", though, we have to create enough safety for ourselves so that we can move out of fight or flight mode, turn back on the powerful potential of our forward-thinking brain, and think about our lives in new ways, instead of the same old ways that we've always done.

We'll explore these ideas further in **Part 3: Reprogram**, where we'll dig deep into mindset shifts and belief rewiring. But first, we're moving into **Part 2:**

Regulate, where we'll learn how to calm and regulate your nervous system—your "hardware"—so it's no longer overheated. With this foundation in place, you'll have the capacity to do the deeper work of reprogramming.

Part 2:

REGULATE

Chapter 6

Regulate: Rebooting Your System

"You can have the best software out there, but it means nothing without the hardware to run it."

Remember how we talked about your logical, problem-solving brain during burnout? It's like trying to get a car to run on fumes—it's just not happening. When you're in burnout mode, your ability to think clearly, plan effectively, or solve problems is basically out the window. Before you can even start reprogramming your subconscious or training your brain to think differently, there's a crucial step you need to take: **getting out of that relentless fight-or-flight loop**. In short, we need to **regulate your nervous system**.

Think of it like rebooting a sluggish computer. When your laptop's frozen because it's trying to juggle too many tabs and tasks, the first thing you do is restart it, right? Nervous system regulation works the same way. It resets your brain and body, getting everything back online and running at full speed.

As we've discussed in earlier chapters, your brain works like a **living, breathing computer**. You've got hardware—the physical brain and nervous system—and software—the beliefs, habits, and subconscious programming that shape your reality. But what happens when this "computer" is overwhelmed or overloaded with stress?

When too many programs (i.e. stressors) are running, your system crashes. Your brain becomes sluggish, unable to process information effectively. Forget focus, problem-solving, or creative thinking—your brain simply doesn't have the capacity. And, if you start trying to rewire all those limiting beliefs while your brain is in this frazzled state, it's like trying to install new software on a computer that's frozen. Your brain's just not ready. Nothing will change because your system isn't working optimally. This isn't just a nice little bonus —it's *foundational* for making lasting changes.

In this chapter, we'll dive into why nervous system regulation matters so much and how it sets the stage for reprogramming the subconscious. The good news is that there's a *lot* of information and a wide variety of strategies and habits out there for nervous system regulation. The bad news is that, with so much information, it can become more complicated than it has to be. To simplify things a bit, think of regulation as the **"pause button"** on your stress response that allows you to come back to center before those ripple effects begin to control your next thoughts and actions.

In the name of simplicity, we're going to cover regulation in a single chapter. Rather than overwhelm your already exhausted brain with all of the nitty gritty details, my goal is to explain both the "what" and the "why" in terms that don't overcomplicate what can oftentimes seem like a foreign language. To start, let's set the foundation for why regulation even matters.

Why Regulation Matters

There's three main reasons why nervous system regulation is a such crucial part of the work before you try to reprogram *anything*:

Reason 1: You Can't Think Clearly When You're in Survival Mode

When your brain is in survival mode, it doesn't have the bandwidth to focus on self-reflection or challenging your system of subconscious beliefs because it cannot access the parts necessary for meaningful growth. It's locked in tunnel vision mode. There's no energy for these things because the stress response diverts all its energy to immediate survival. Your prefrontal cortex—the logical, future-planning part of your brain—gets cut off from the blood flow it needs to function properly, while your amygdala (the brain's alarm system) takes control and your nervous system sends all that energy and blood flow to your body for the sympathetic nervous system response.

The result? You can't think long-term, problem-solve, or see the bigger picture. Without regulation, your brain is essentially in lockdown mode, focused on handling perceived threats rather than allowing space for growth. Nervous system regulation helps you escape this loop and regain access to your prefrontal cortex, so you can engage with deeper work like reprogramming.

Reason 2: Regulation Is Key to Intentional Neuroplasticity

We've already discussed neuroplasticity—the brain's ability to reshape itself based on new experiences. Neuroplasticity works best when your brain is regulated. When you're in a calm state, your brain is primed to create new neural pathways, absorbing new information and learning from it. On the flip side, when you're in fight-or-flight mode, your brain defaults to its **subconscious programming**, relying on outdated beliefs and automated responses. Without finding that pause button that exists between your interpretation and response, you're more likely to revert to those outdated, subconscious automated responses based on your past. It's only when you regulate your nervous system that your brain can move from survival mode to growth mode. This shift opens the door for real change, allowing you to rewrite old, limiting beliefs and pave the way for new ones.

Reason 3: Without Regulation, You Reinforce Stress-Based Programming

Stress is a loop. Every time your brain responds to a stressor without regulation, it reinforces the neural pathways that keep you stuck in a stress-based mindset. It filters reality through a lens of fear or danger, making it harder and harder to escape that cycle. Without regulation, every stressor you experience only serves to hardwire stress-based thinking deeper into your brain. Regulation breaks this loop. By calming your nervous system, you create space for new patterns to emerge. Instead of hardwiring stress, you're rewiring for balance, safety, and calm.

Regulating your nervous system gives your brain a chance to experience calm and safety, which is necessary for rewiring old beliefs and programming. When you reboot your hardware, you give your brain the opportunity to operate at its full potential. The outcome isn't just to calm you down— the bigger outcome is to turn back on the full power of your logical, creative, thinking brain.

The Pause Button: Creating Space to Respond Instead of React

Remember that flowchart of how your brain processes reality under chronic burnout? It's a constant loop that keeps running on autopilot, influenced by subconscious patterns and stress triggers. But what if you could stop that loop, even just for a moment? This is where **regulation** comes in, giving you the power to hit a pause button before the brain runs the same cycle again.

1. Input
2. Subconscious Filtering
3. Interpretation

4. Response
5. Reinforcement

With regulation, you learn how to create a moment of pause that exists between the interpretation and response to interrupt the repeat cycle. If we can figure out how to pause that program from running on autopilot, based on past patterns, we can then work on creating a sense of safety so that our thinking brain can take action from conscious intention, instead of subconscious reaction.

That moment of pause is crucial. Instead of letting your **amygdala** (the brain's alarm system) take over and automatically react to *perceived* danger, you get to consciously choose your response. It's an opportunity to let your **prefrontal cortex** (your logical, future-planning brain) step in and assess the situation with a clear head.

And even if you miss it in the moment, regulation can help reverse the effects of stress afterward. If you can catch yourself in the midst of experiencing the rock splash, you have a lot more power and control to manage (and even prevent) the ripples. But even if the ripples have already taken hold of your mind, regulating can slow and calm them down, resetting you back to center.

So what exactly does that pause button look like? How do you reset and reboot the hardware? How do we calm down the brain's **fight-or-flight** response and regain access to clear, logical thinking? Let's explore some *simple* techniques that can help you make this pause a habit, giving you the space to choose intentional responses instead of falling into automatic reactions. Think of this as nervous system regulation, *without all the fluff*!

The Three Forms of Regulation

Regulation comes in three main forms: **physical, mental, and emotional**. These three components make up your current inner state, and when we change one, we change all three. At the core of all three forms of regulation is the idea that your inner state—the way you feel physically, mentally, and emotionally—dictates how much control your prefrontal cortex has over your amygdala. Nervous system regulation turns down the dial on your emotional brain, allowing the thinking brain to regain control.

The calmer you are, the more your logical, future-focused brain can run the show. The more stressed or overwhelmed you are, the more your survival instincts (your amygdala and programmed responses) take over. Essentially, the goal is to create more safety from the inside out. What does internal safety actually meant though?

From a neuropsychological perspective, **safety** is the state in which your brain and body feel protected from threat, and your nervous system is in balance. Only when you feel safe can you truly access your higher thinking capabilities, engage in creative problem-solving, and experience emotional healing.

So, let's break down each form of regulation and look at some simple strategies that can help you shift your inner state. This isn't an exhaustive list, and you've likely heard of many of these techniques—or even practice some of them already. My goal is to make sure that you know the "why" so that you can make these habits your own, without losing the true value.

- **Physical regulation** involves using your body to tell the brain, "Hey, it's okay. You're safe." This signals the parasympathetic nervous system to take over, bringing the body and brain back into balance. Think of this as hitting the reset button at a biological level, allowing the brain's operating system to switch out of "panic mode" and into a state where it can think clearly again. Here's a few simple strategies for physical regulation:

    1. **Deep Diaphragmatic Breathing**

        ✓ **Why it works:** Deep breathing activates the **PNS (rest and relax)**, signaling to your brain that you are safe. By focusing on slow, controlled breaths that expand the diaphragm, you stimulate your **vagus nerve** (a key player in the parasympathetic response), lower your heart rate, and reduce cortisol levels. This counters the stress response and helps calm the amygdala, allowing your prefrontal cortex to regain control. Research by Gerritsen and Band (2018) supports how slow-paced breathing exercises can improve nervous system balance if you're interested in the nitty gritty![1]

✓ **How it works:**
- Find a comfortable seat or lie down.
- Place one hand on your chest and the other on your abdomen.
- Inhale deeply through your nose, letting your abdomen and chest rise as you fill your lungs.
- Exhale slowly through your mouth, imagining breathing out through a small straw. Pursing your lips will help you extend your exhale.
- Repeat as needed until you start to feel centered and calm.

2. **Progressive Muscle Relaxation (PMR)**

✓ **Why it works:** Stress creates physical tension in your body, which can keep your nervous system stuck in sympathetic mode (fight-or-flight). PMR reduces this tension by helping you gradually relax each muscle group, signaling to your brain that the threat is over. It also helps you identify areas where stress is still being held, giving you the opportunity to release that tension, and reconnect the brain to the body.

✓ **How it works:**
- Start at your feet and work your way up to the top of your head.
- Tense each muscle group for a few seconds and then slowly release the tension.
- Focus on how your muscles feel as you let go of the tightness with each exhale.

---

[1] Gerritsen, R. J., & Band, G. P. H. (2018). Breath of life: The respiratory vagal stimulation model of contemplative activity. *Frontiers in Human Neuroscience, 12,* 397.

- Move through each body part, from your feet to your face, breathing deeply and relaxing your muscles.
- Once you reach the top of your body, you can reverse the process to circle back to any parts that may have tensed up again.

3. **Shake it Out (literally any sort of physical activity)**

   ✓ **Why it works:** Physical activity triggers the release of endorphins, dopamine, and serotonin, all of which reduce stress and balance cortisol. It also lowers adrenaline, helping to restore equilibrium to your nervous system. Think about it this way—the more you move your body, the faster that built-up cortisol and adrenaline moves through your system. Shaking out stress is a natural response we see in animals after they experience a threat. Unfortunately, humans have been conditioned to suppress this instinct, but it's time to give ourselves permission again to shake it off!

   ✓ **How it works:**
   - Engage in any form of exercise, whether it's a brisk walk, a full workout, or just taking a moment to "shake it off".
   - If you're low on energy or time, try a quick 2-5 minute burst of shaking your body out.
   - Start from your legs and work your way up through your torso and arms, shaking off the tension.
   - Don't be afraid to get silly! You can even add a loud yell or a dance to the mix—just like a child shaking off stress during a tantrum. Let go and let your body release that pent-up energy.

- **Mental regulation** is all about giving your mind a break from the chaos of overwhelming thoughts and reducing the cognitive load it has to process. This is like allowing your brain to reset its filters, helping your brain to work more in your favor. Here are a few of my favorite strategies to give yourself a bit of a mental brain break:

1. **Micro-tasking and Microbreaks**

    ✓ **Why it works:** When you're stressed, large tasks or looming deadlines can send your brain into overdrive, making it hard to focus. **Micro-tasking**—breaking tasks into small, manageable steps—reduces cognitive overload and re-engages the **prefrontal cortex**, the part of the brain responsible for logical thinking. Research by Mark et al. (2014) supports the benefits of chunking tasks, showing that this method reduces perceived stress.[2] Taking intentional **microbreaks** between tasks lets your brain reset and gives the **parasympathetic nervous system** a chance to activate. It's like giving yourself a water break in the middle of a marathon called daily life. All of this helps you to regain a sense of control over that lengthy to-do list.

    ✓ **How it works:**
    - Start with a big goal (e.g., a work project) and break it into smaller, achievable steps.
    - Pick a task that you can complete in 5-10 minutes and focus on that until it's done. Avoid any sort of multi-tasking, as this puts extra pressure on your brain to switch between tasks rapidly.
    - After 30 minutes to an hour, take a 15-minute microbreak —stretch, stand up, or throw a mini dance party. This cycle of short tasks and breaks keeps your mind engaged without overwhelming it.
    - **Bonus points** if you get outside to breathe in fresh air and soak up some sunlight.

---

[2] Mark, G., Gudith, D., & Klocke, U. (2014). The cost of interrupted work: More speed and stress. *Proceedings of the SIGCHI Conference on Human Factors in Computing Systems*, 1071–1080.

2. **Mindfulness Meditation**

    ✓ **Why it works:** When stressed, the brain often fixates on past problems or future fears, both of which activate the **amygdala**. **Mindfulness meditation** helps shift attention back to the present moment, reducing focus on perceived threats and calming the nervous system. Regular mindfulness practice also increases **gray matter** in the **prefrontal cortex**, improving emotional regulation and helping override the amygdala's reactive tendencies. A study by Hölzel et al. (2011) found that after just 8 weeks of mindfulness, participants showed increased gray matter density in areas of the brain related to learning and memory.[3]

    ✓ **How it works:**
    - Sit or lie down comfortably and close your eyes.
    - Focus on your breath as you inhale and exhale, simply observing without trying to change it.
    - If your mind wanders (which it will), gently guide your focus back to your breath. The goal is not to stop your thoughts but to become aware of them without getting caught up.
    - Start with 5-10 minutes a day and increase over time. Bonus points if you listen to a **theta brainwave** meditation playlist while doing this for an added calming effect.

3. **The Two "What Ifs"**

    ✓ **Why it works:** When you're in a stress response, the brain often falls into "what if" scenarios, fixating on worst-case

---

[3] Hölzel, B. K., et al. (2011). "Mindfulness practice leads to increases in regional brain gray matter density." *Psychiatry Research: Neuroimaging,* 191(1), 36-43.

outcomes, which keeps the amygdala in control. This is a natural part of our **negativity bias**, which primes us to focus on danger. However, intentionally introducing a **positive** "what if" scenario can help shift the brain from fear-based thinking to a more balanced perspective. By considering both negative and positive possibilities, you broaden your thinking, reduce tunnel vision, and open up space for creative problem-solving. This also gives the brain space to focus on potential solutions rather than only threats.

✓ **How it works:**
- When you find yourself spiraling into a negative "what if" (e.g., *"What if I fail?"*), counter it by introducing a positive "what if" (e.g., *"What if this turns out better than expected?"*).
- Balancing both perspectives helps break the cycle of catastrophic thinking and opens up mental space for solutions.
- **Bonus tip:** When you're stuck in a negative "what if," challenge the narrative by asking, **"What do I know to be 100% true about this?"** This helps the **prefrontal cortex** take back more control, giving you a more logical perspective on whether your fears are based on facts or assumptions.

- **Emotional Regulation** helps manage the waves of emotion that stress triggers, preventing your emotions from hijacking your rational brain. When emotions run high, they can hijack your brain's ability to respond rationally. This involves acknowledging the emotions you're experiencing without being overwhelmed by them. This rewires the brain to process emotions with more logic and less reaction. Here's a few simple strategies to regulate your emotional state:

1. **Give it a Name**

    ✓ **Why it works:** Labeling emotions shifts activity from the reactive amygdala to the analytical prefrontal cortex. This simple act creates mental space between you and your emotions, allowing you to process feelings more objectively, allowing you to better understand what you're feeling without the emotional reaction taking complete control.

    ✓ **How it works:**
    - Pause and ask, "What exactly am I feeling right now?"
    - Use specific labels instead of vague terms—are you anxious, frustrated, or overwhelmed?
    - Once you identify the emotion, acknowledge it without judgment.
    - Get curious about it—whether or not you understand the root cause is fine. The goal is to process the feeling logically rather than reactively.
    - Find more acceptance with the emotion by normalizing it with yourself. For example, you could say, "No wonder I'm feeling stressed." Talk to yourself about your feelings like you'd speak to your younger self!

2. **Journaling for Emotional Expression**

    ✓ **Why it works:** Writing about your emotions is a form of emotional release. The word "emotion" comes from the Greek term emotere, which translates to "energy in motion." Journaling provides an outlet to process and release uncomfortable emotional energy, which prevents them from being bottled up and intensifying the stress response. When you journal, you give structure and form to your emotions. The "energy in motion" becomes matter when we write it down. This practice helps to reduce the emotional charge over time and promote emotional resilience.

✓ **How it works:**
- Set a timer for 5–10 minutes to write freely about your emotions.
- Start with prompts like *"I feel..."* or *"I'm struggling with..."* to get the words flowing.
- Don't worry about grammar, structure, or coherence—the goal is emotional release, not polished prose.
- After writing, review what you've captured and reflect on any patterns or insights.

3. **Positive Self-Talk**

    ✓ **Why it works:** Negative self-talk triggers the brain's threat response, keeping the amygdala in overdrive. Positive self-talk acts as an antivirus, soothing the amygdala and re-engaging the prefrontal cortex. By practicing self-compassion, you signal safety to your brain and focus on solutions instead of self-criticism. If you wouldn't say it to your best friend, child, or partner, don't say it to yourself! Your mind is always listening to you. When you consciously choose to speak kindly and encouragingly to yourself, you're giving your brain new inputs that can positive affect the filtering process.

    ✓ **How it works:**
    - When you catch yourself thinking negatively, pause and notice your inner dialogue.
    - Ask yourself, *"Would I say this to someone I love?"* If not, replace it with kinder words.
    - Counter negativity with compassionate statements like: "This is hard, but many people feel this way when facing challenges." or "I'm doing the best I can with the resources I have right now."
    - Repeat positive affirmations to train your brain to focus on supportive thoughts over time. This simple act of

kindness toward yourself helps soothe the emotional distress, while not gaslighting your situation.

Now that you understand the importance of regulation and exactly what it all means, you can see why it's the first critical step in shifting out of burnout and into growth mode. Once you've reset your system and created more internal safety, you can begin to work on reprogramming those deeply embedded beliefs and creating lasting change without fear getting in your way.

As a reminder, this is just a short list of options. If it doesn't work for you, don't try to force it. You, and only you, know what brings you the most peace and calm. Don't get too caught up in everyone else's definition of regulation if it doesn't work for your unique mind, brain, and body. Remember the root purpose— to turn back on the powerful potential of your logical, future-planning brain to think about and do things in a new way. Without a regulated brain, we can't access the part of our mind that allows us to reprogram deeply embedded beliefs and create new neural pathways.

The Brain Craves Routine

Remember our simplified definition of stress? It's a natural reaction to unexpected change. And while there's a lot of unexpected changes that we're faced with on a daily basis that we *can't* control, we do have control over our own routines. Having a predictable routine that our brain can rely on during times of uncertainty and stress becomes a strong foundation and pillars of support that we can lean on to keep ourselves more protected from any unexpected changes or circumstances that may come our way.

A good routine, to start with, might look like going to bed and waking up at about the same time everyday so that your circadian rhythms start becoming more balanced and consistent. It might be carving out a half-day to yourself every Sunday to simply rest and recharge. You could stop there and be better off already, but now that you know the power of nervous system regulation, you have a unique opportunity to create a new, purposeful routine for yourself that allows you to create more physical, mental, and emotional regulation on a consistent basis.

Now, let's be real. If you end up reading over all of this without actually implementing, it becomes awareness without action. So rather than wait until tomorrow to start creating healthier habits and routines, I highly encourage you to use this as an opportunity to craft a balanced routine that works for you! It doesn't have to be anything fancy. You can always add to this routine as you find the energy and capacity, but start *something* today!

Below is a planning template to get you started. The habits and strategies have been broken down into the three categories of regulation we've already discussed. Perhaps pick just one new habit that you'll start today, and then choose 1-2 others that you'll add into the mix as your brain begins to realize that it's safe enough to try something else new.

After you've completed this first critical step of regulation, you'll be ready to begin the much deeper work of reprogramming your subconscious and stepping into the future you desire and deserve!

New Habits/Strategies I'm Going to Adopt:

Physical Regulation:

- [ ] Deep Diaphragmatic Breathing
- [ ] Progressive Muscle Relaxation
- [ ] Exercise (Shaking it Out)
- [ ] My Own: _____

Mental Regulation:

- ☐ Micro-tasking/Microbreaks
- ☐ Mindfulness Meditation
- ☐ The Two "What Ifs"
- ☐ My Own: _____

Emotional Regulation:

- ☐ "Give It A Name"
- ☐ Journaling
- ☐ Positive Self-Talk
- ☐ My Own: _____

Part 3:

REPROGRAM

Chapter 7

Reprogram: Understanding Conditioning & Programming

"Beliefs are simply illusions of repeated perceptions."

As tempting as it might be to dive straight into the inner work of reprogramming and rewiring, it's crucial to pause and understand what's happening beneath the surface, at a subconscious level. Skipping this foundational step is like rebooting a computer with corrupted code—it might run smoother for a moment, but those underlying issues will inevitably resurface.

The same applies to your brain. If you don't uncover the subconscious beliefs and programming driving your actions, any attempt at change will only scratch the surface. Those deeper, unseen programs will keep running the show, and you'll likely find yourself stuck in the same patterns, wondering why nothing has really changed. I tell you this from lived experience!

You've already learned about how burnout takes hold, but to escape it, it will help to understand how those subconscious programs that create our "software" and influence our response to stress are formed in the first place. In this chapter, we'll dig deep into the origins of your subconscious conditioning, unraveling the story of how your beliefs, habits, and reactions were shaped. It's not just about identifying what's not working—it's about understanding *why* it exists in the first place, so you can begin to reprogram the operating system of your mind.

The Software: How the Programs Are Created

Remember, your brain is an incredibly powerful, living, breathing supercomputer. While the hardware—the physical brain—might seem solid and fixed, the software—the subconscious beliefs running beneath the surface—has been programmed over time and is constantly being updated, often without your conscious awareness.

The tricky part? Most of this programming was installed before you even had the awareness to question it. By the time you were seven years old, much of your subconscious belief system—your "truths" about work, success, rest, and life in general—was already taking shape. During these early years, your brain predominantly operated in a **theta brainwave state**, which is a highly suggestible state. In this state, everything you saw, heard, and experienced was absorbed as truth without filtering or analysis (Meyer et al., 2019).[1] It's like being in a constant state of learning, without the ability, yet, for critical analysis.

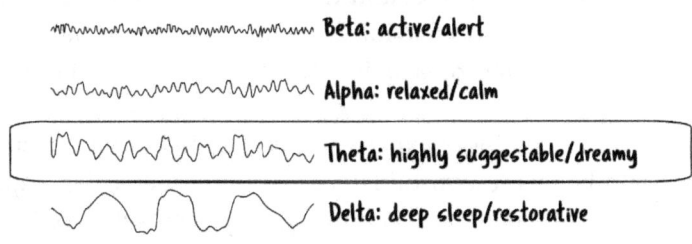

---

[1] Meyer, M., Endedijk, H. M., Van Ede, F., & Hunnius, S. (2019). Theta oscillations in 4-year-olds are sensitive to task engagement and task demands. *Scientific Reports*, 9(1). https://doi.org/10.1038/s41598-019-42615-x

Theta brainwaves are typically associated with deep meditation, hypnosis, and the dreamy state just before falling asleep. In this state, your brain is like a sponge, taking in every interaction, every modeled behavior, and every spoken word as raw data. The world around you becomes your blueprint for how things are "supposed to be." If your brain is a computer, then these younger years are the equivalent of the initial coding that creates your foundational framework through which you perceive and interact with the world.

Fast-forward to adulthood, and these subconscious programs are still running the show. You might find yourself working long hours, feeling guilty about taking breaks, or pushing past your limits—not necessarily because it's what you want, but because your subconscious has been wired to believe it's the only way to succeed.

These deeply ingrained beliefs were formed early on, reinforced over time, and validated by life experiences that seemed to confirm them. In essence, your brain took the blueprint it was given as a child and used it to navigate the adult world. The result? You may now be operating from outdated or unhelpful programming, chasing dreams or goals that might not even be your own.

The Software: How the Programs Adapt

Our brains are highly **adaptive**, and they're also **pattern-seeking**. The more we experience a particular behavior or belief, the more it becomes hardwired into the brain through neuroplasticity. Repetition is the key here.

As we gather more and more experiences in our lives that are similar to each other, the brain begins to consolidate all of these memories, especially those with a strong emotional association, into generalized subconscious beliefs. It's the equivalent of taking a bunch of files on your laptop and putting them into a zip folder. The more evidence your brain finds to back up these beliefs over the course of your life experiences, the more hardwired they become. At first, there might be a bigger gap between your interpretation and response, as your brain searches through those multiple "files" of previous memories to make sense of your reality. But, as you create more memories from similar experiences, the time it takes for your brain to create an internal interpretation and respond decreases. As the program becomes stronger and more hardwired, your responses become more and more habituated.

For example, if you grew up in a home where success was equated with hard work and productivity, your brain likely wired itself to associate your worth with being busy or achieving something. If you continued to hear messages or saw behavior modeled that rest is lazy, that repeated record eventually becomes a belief. Over time, repeated evidence—like praise for working late or guilt for taking a break—solidified that belief. Now, as an adult, you might find yourself struggling to rest without guilt or pushing past your limits because your subconscious is still running on the outdated programming that says rest equals laziness.

This worked out to our benefit at one time. If it weren't for our subconscious beliefs, then it would take our brains too much time to consciously process what to do in the case of a tiger jumping out of the bushes. By using our subconscious programming, we're able to respond much more quickly. It's an efficiency model that serves us in certain ways, especially when faced with threats.

This is where the subconscious mind's power becomes most evident. Unlike the conscious brain, which analyzes and reasons, the subconscious acts as an autopilot. It runs in the background, guiding your thoughts, actions, and behaviors based on the beliefs it absorbed and strengthened. As a matter of fact, it's estimated that 90-95% of your perception of reality comes from the subconscious. Only about 5% is conscious thought. This means that while you might consciously *want* to change, your subconscious programming often pulls you back into old patterns because it overpowers the conscious self.

The challenge? These beliefs aren't always helpful or accurate when there's no tiger in the bushes. When faced with a situation, your brain filters the experience through the beliefs it's already stored, determining whether to activate a stress response or not. And because the brain tends to prioritize negative experiences (hello, again, negativity bias), many of the beliefs driving your behavior are rooted in fear, stress, or avoidance.

If your brain filters reality through these deeply ingrained beliefs, they essentially become the operating instructions for your life. They direct your brain's "algorithm" to focus on information that reinforces those beliefs while filtering out anything that contradicts them. Just like the software that runs a computer, your subconscious programming runs the show of your life in the background without you having much conscious awareness of it. This is exactly why our subconscious programming has such a strong grip on our lives.

It all goes back to the fact that your brain's main job is to keep you alive and safe. And one of the ways that it does this is by creating shortcuts that saves your brain energy that can then be used on other things in case it's needed (like your repeat fight or flight response). Your brain is always looking for ways to be more efficient, and beliefs are one of its key tools for achieving this. Put simply, beliefs help us create meaning out of our daily lives.

To move forward in life, especially if you're feeling stuck in a cycle of chronic stress, it's essential to recognize that many of the patterns you operate from—patterns that push you into burnout—are deeply rooted in childhood conditioning. They're not conscious choices; they're automatic responses based on beliefs formed early on. Even if you were never told explicitly, *"You must work constantly to be successful,"* messages like "Resting means I'm lazy" or "I'm only valuable when I'm productive" likely became embedded in your subconscious. Your brain, in a theta state at the time, didn't have the ability to question these beliefs; it simply absorbed them. Over time, they become the foundation of your belief system and dictate your behavior, often without you even realizing it.

You've likely spent years, if not decades, running on this subconscious programming. Now that you're aware of how deep these beliefs go, you're in a much better position to start changing them. The way your brain is wired today isn't random—it's the result of years of conditioning, programming, and reinforcement. And, unless you've taken the time to examine and challenge these beliefs, they'll continue to drive your behavior and perceptions, keeping you stuck in the same patterns that keep you doing the same things over and over again expecting different results. As the saying goes, doing the same thing over and over expecting different results is the very definition of **insanity**.

Understanding how these beliefs were formed is essential to changing them, but understanding the effect they have on you *now* and how they affect your perception of reality at this very moment should provide a bit more motivation for the upcoming inner work of rewiring and reprogramming.

Chapter 8

Reprogram: The Effects of Conditioning & Programming

"The subconscious sabotages your growth and potential by canceling its possibility."

In the last chapter, we explored how early childhood conditioning and brain development set the stage for many of your subconscious beliefs. Up until the age of about 7 years old, your brain was in a highly impressionable theta state, absorbing everything around you like a sponge. The beliefs formed during this time are still running the show today, often without your conscious awareness.

Now, in this chapter, we're going to dig deeper into how those subconscious beliefs—formed in your most malleable years—continue to shape how you react to stress and manage life's pressures. You'll begin to see how your programming, particularly around work, productivity, and stress, is likely fueling the thoughts and behaviors that push you into burnout. We'll also dive into how repeated stress responses create neural pathways that reinforce these burnout behaviors, making them feel almost automatic.

Instead of exhausting ourselves trying to control everything outside of our control—the economy, the job market, or the general stress of life—we're going to focus on the one thing we can actually change: **our mind**. By understanding how our subconscious beliefs and neural pathways influence our reactions, we can take back the reins and finally get unstuck!

Fleas, Elephants, and Us: The Power of Conditioning

There's a well-known psychology experiment that illustrates conditioning best. If you put a bunch of fleas in a jar with a lid, the fleas will try again and again to jump out, until they finally learn that jumping too high only leads to bumping their little flea heads. A few days later, you can take the lid off of the jar, but the fleas will not jump out. They will only jump below the height of the lid— not because they can't actually jump out, but because they've been conditioned to believe that it's not possible.

A similar phenomenon happens with elephants raised in captivity. As babies, the elephants get chained up by one of their legs to a stake in the ground. As much as they try and try to break free from the strong chains as babies, they eventually succumb to the fact that this is just how it is. When they become adults, with enough strength to easily break through that same chain, they don't even try. They've been conditioned to believe they're powerless.

Not only are these scenarios a form of learned helplessness, but they are very real examples of how conditioning becomes the very thing that holds us back when we are, indeed, perfectly capable of different results. Humans aren't too different from those fleas or elephants. We are raised to believe certain things that become our source of truth over time. These "truths" often go unquestioned because they become so ingrained in us that we forget or fail to see any other possibilities.

When you're in burnout mode, your brain flips to this same sort of autopilot mode, where all of these subconscious directions, created by your conditioning, are stored. Your conscious mind—the part responsible for logic, planning, and decision-making—doesn't have the required energy to do its job effectively. That's when your subconscious takes the wheel. The prefrontal cortex, where higher-level thinking happens, is tapped out, so your brain defaults to energy-efficient patterns from your past, stored in the subconscious. It's like having a GPS in your brain quietly navigating based on old maps—even if you've consciously set a new destination. It's this autopilot mode that, so often, creates our reality, without us even realizing it.

The Matrix *IS* Your Mind

Right at this very moment, your brain is trying to process an unimaginable amount of data. Every sound, sensation, and image is hitting your brain like a tsunami. Your brain can only consciously handle less than 0.001% of that data from one second to the next, though. That's where your brain's built-in algorithm comes in, deciding what gets through and what gets tossed. This personal assistant for your brain is influenced by your focus, needs, and, most importantly, your subconscious beliefs.

For example, if you buy a new car and suddenly notice that same make and model everywhere, it's not because the universe magically multiplied those cars. Your brain's filtering system has flagged this detail as important after you spent hours researching and thinking about it. This filtering happens automatically based on what your brain has been primed to focus on. You might find yourself wondering, "were all these cars not here before?" It's not that your car twins weren't there before. It's just that they weren't in your **awareness** before.

Here's the tough pill to swallow: you're not experiencing "reality." You're experiencing your brain's *filtered version* of it. What you see, hear, and perceive as "reality" is just a processed, pieced-together interpretation of sensory input. That huge packet of 11 million bits of data hits our brain, and we do our darnedest to try to make sense of it before the next packet of data.

Because we can't possibly process all 11 million bits at once, our filtering system decides which ~50 bits to filter to the conscious brain. Then, to fill in the other pieces of the "whole", our brain uses what we already have stored in the subconscious to create an interpretation of that data that makes sense to us. It's like a puzzle where half of the pieces are missing, and your brain has to guess what the "whole" puzzle would look like. At the end of the day, we call this "output" our reality.

So how does your brain decide what makes the cut? Surprise, surprise, this is also influenced by our subconscious beliefs. While the "algorithm" (aka the filtering system) helps your brain decide what sensory information to process, it's your beliefs that also guide how that information *is* or *is not* processed and interpreted.

For instance, if you hold the belief, *"I have to work harder than everyone else to be successful,"* your brain will ignore or dismiss evidence that contradicts it. Similarly, if you believe, *"I need to stay busy to be productive,"* any downtime will be interpreted as lazy, unproductive, and your brain will interpret rest as wasted time. As you can imagine, this distorted perception of reality can further exacerbate burnout for us. Even if you see evidence that people can succeed without burning themselves out, your brain will ignore or dismiss that information because it doesn't align with your deeply held belief.

You might find yourself saying, *"I'll rest after this project,"* or *"Just a little more time and hard work, and then I'll relax."* These autopilot responses stem from subconscious programming. And when you're burned out, they kick in full force. Every time you respond the same way, your brain strengthens the neural pathways that link stress to overwork. The more you repeat this cycle, the more automatic it becomes. This is why burnout feels so overwhelming—it's not just a mental state, but a neurological loop reinforcing itself.

In other words, burnout can become a **stress addiction**. If that term feels heavy, think of it as a "burnout loop." Every time you ignore your body's signals and push through exhaustion, you reinforce the belief that rest is only earned when you feel worthy of it. And when your worth is rooted in your level of busyness and productivity, you talk yourself into a reality where you use your level of stress as your indication for rest. Over time, breaking the loop feels more and more impossible because your brain clings to these patterns as a survival mechanism.

Your brain isn't trying to keep you miserable. It's just a little overcommitted to the hustle. It's like that friend that won't stop giving you advice, even though you never asked for it. Because your brain is filtering reality to support your belief that rest is unproductive or that you haven't earned it yet, you don't even notice that your body is screaming for a break. You miss the signs of fatigue, and instead, you double down on your efforts to stay busy, therefore reinforcing the "software."

Even when you tell yourself that you're going to do things differently (the input), the subconscious mind talks you out of it because it doesn't fit with the current system of beliefs (output). Another way to think about this is that your conscious brain is the "goal setter" and your subconscious mind is the "goal getter." You might have the grandest goals for yourself, but if your subconscious isn't programmed to accept those goals as a possibility for you, it will continue to hold you back.

It's why manifestation might seem like a cosmic joke that works for everyone else but you. Here's the catch: you're giving your brain directions that contradict its programming. Your brain's like, *"Wait, you want to rest, succeed, and have balance? LOL, I don't think you know me."*

The Goal Setter vs. The Goal Getter

Your subconscious has a tendency to sabotage your growth and potential by canceling the possibility of it. This is why manifestation just doesn't seem to work out for so many people. It's because you're trying to give your brain a set of directions that completely goes against its programming and wiring. It simply doesn't know how to make that happen when your beliefs contradict it.

Let's try a quick experiment to illustrate how your brain's filtering system works. Look around your space and find three things that are round. Easy, right? Now, see if you can find three things that are both round and red. This might be more challenging. If you nailed it, congrats—your brain's filter is in full working order. It followed your directions and served up confirmation of what you were looking for. If not, no worries; just wait. Later today, you might spot a red rubber ball on a playground and think, *"Aha, round and red!"* That's your brain doing its thing: following the instructions you gave it and scanning for evidence that fits.

Now, imagine applying this concept to your beliefs. Instead of defaulting to, *"I have to grind to be successful,"* you shift to, *"Success can be easy and fulfilling."* Just like spotting red-round things, your brain would begin identifying evidence to back up that belief. Sounds simple, right? Not so fast.

When it comes to changing your path and living on different terms than you have your entire life, things aren't so straightforward. Remember, your subconscious mind filters out anything that doesn't align with its pre-existing beliefs. You might *consciously* want to live a balanced, peaceful life, but your *subconscious* is all about those hardwired "truths" it's picked up from past experiences—truths like, *"Rest is lazy,"* or, *"Busyness equals success."* These ingrained beliefs block new ideas from taking root and it's why the moment you sit down to rest, those subconscious whispers chime in: *"Shouldn't you be doing something more productive right now?"*

The subconscious doesn't care if a belief serves you or not. Its sole purpose is to keep you safe and conserve energy. It does this by automating responses based on what you've experienced repeatedly. Your subconscious mind will only surface evidence that aligns with your existing beliefs and what you've been most prone to focus on *up until now*.

For millennials, this often leads to what psychologists call **cognitive dissonance**: the clash between what you consciously want (e.g., rest, balance, success without burnout) and what your subconscious has been programmed to believe (e.g., rest is lazy, busyness equals success). Again, this is to be expected, because our subconscious creates upwards of 90% of our perception of reality. You didn't *consciously* decide to believe that burnout is the only path to success, but because of your programming, it's become the default mode your brain operates in. This is the nature of conditioning.

You can tell yourself *"I'm worthy of rest and peace,"* but if your subconscious isn't wired for that, it's going to call BS on you and that affirmation of yours becomes powerless. Why would your brain even waste the energy of filtering in data that doesn't fit with what you believe to even be true? Your mind sees this as incredibly inefficient, so it filters it out before you even have a chance to become conscious of its existence.

These limiting beliefs don't just trap you in burnout—they amplify your stress. If you believe you always have to be productive, moments of rest trigger guilt or anxiety, adding even more stress to the pile. Your subconscious is sabotaging your peace by layering these limiting beliefs over every situation. If you've faced financial instability, job insecurity, or other common millennial challenges, your brain has likely stored these as trauma. When new stressors arise, your subconscious links them to those past traumas, making today's struggles feel even heavier than they actually are.

That's why it's so important to do the inner work first. Sure, you could tell yourself again and again *"I'm ready for more balance,"* but it's no match for the 95% of you operating on autopilot. Creating lasting change requires reprogramming the thing that's creating the large majority of our perception of reality!

Remember, burnout isn't just a product of your current environment—it's the result of deeply ingrained subconscious patterns that have been reinforced over time. The next step is to become aware of these patterns in your day-to-day life. Start noticing when you're defaulting to automatic responses and ask yourself: *"What belief is driving this behavior? Is it serving me, or is it keeping me stuck?"* Start getting curious, instead of resistant, so that you can start working *with* your subconscious mind, instead of against it.

Life either happens to you or for you, and the algorithm can ebb and flow between one or the other. If your beliefs are empowering and aligned with what you want to achieve, they can help you navigate life more easily. But if your beliefs are outdated or rooted in outdated programming, they can keep you stuck in patterns that no longer serve you. While they were *originally* formed to keep you safe, they might now be keeping you stuck.

The more you can recognize these patterns, the more power you have to change them. Remember, your brain's filtering system is automatic, but it's not unchangeable. Once you become aware of how your beliefs are shaping your perception of reality, you can start to challenge those beliefs and create new, healthier patterns.

As we go forward, remember: change isn't just about breaking free from old beliefs. It's about installing new ones that truly align with the life you want, based on your own terms instead of the ones you were conditioned to believe.

Chapter 9

Reprogram: Taking Inventory of Your Beliefs

"Whatever we plant in the gardens of our mind and feed with repetition and emotion will, one day, become reality."

By now, you've learned how your brain works, how societal pressures have shaped your beliefs, and how subconscious programs drive your everyday reality. Here's where things get exciting: it's time to turn that knowledge into action. It's time to shift from learning to **DOING**!

Before you can reprogram the beliefs that are no longer serving you, we need to identify them first. This chapter will guide you through a hands-on exercise to uncover the beliefs driving your habits and choices. You'll assess each belief and decide if it's worth keeping, needs to be let go of, or if it's time to create a new one. Think of this as a mental "spring cleaning" that clears away limiting beliefs and sets the foundation for a healthier, more balanced mindset.

Identifying Your Limiting Beliefs

Beliefs act as the foundation for how you perceive the world. Some of these beliefs serve you well, pushing you toward growth and fulfillment. But others? They keep you stuck in burnout, stress, and self-doubt. By identifying your core beliefs, you're effectively hacking into your brain's algorithm—bringing these automatic programs into conscious awareness so you can decide what serves you and what doesn't.

We'll get to creating new, more positive beliefs later, but based on our negativity bias, we know that it's oftentimes easier to identify what we *don't* want first. Let's start with some common limiting beliefs, especially among millennials, to see if any resonate with you.

Take some time to check off the ones that feel familiar, and add any of your own in the blank spaces.

- ☐ "I have to work harder than others to be successful."
- ☐ "Rest is laziness."
- ☐ "I'm only valuable when I'm productive."
- ☐ "I can't say no, because others will be disappointed."
- ☐ "I don't have time to take care of myself."
- ☐ "I'll never be able to catch up to my peers."
- ☐ "Success requires sacrifice, even if it means going beyond my limit."
- ☐ _____
- ☐ _____

These are the beliefs that may have been formed during your upbringing, shaped by societal expectations, or influenced by your own experiences. They are often so deeply ingrained that we don't even realize we're operating under their influence.

While you may resonate with many, or all, of these limiting beliefs, let's start by identifying the one that is keeping you the most stuck! Oftentimes, we can identify these super sticky beliefs because they come with a "but".

Ask yourself what you want more of in life. Often, when we state our desires, the hidden "but" sneaks in, revealing those self-limiting narratives. The best way to uncover hidden limiting beliefs is to listen to what comes after the word "**but**" in your thoughts.

What's Your "But"?

- Begin by making a list of what you actually ***do*** want more of in your life, and see what comes up for you after the "but".

    - I want more peace and joy, but _____

    - I want more financial freedom and abundance, but _____

    - I want more _____, but _____

- Whatever you fill in after the "but" can give you clues to those limiting beliefs that are holding you back the most. For example:
    - *"I want more peace, but I have too many responsibilities."*
    - This might point to a belief like "I can only have peace once everything else is handled."

- Based on your *"but"*, what might be the limiting belief(s) that are hiding behind this?

_____

_____

_____

Tracing the Origins of Your Limiting Belief

Most of our beliefs take root in childhood, shaped by experiences, authority figures, and societal messages. By reflecting on their origins, you can begin to identify where the conditioning came from in the first place. We'll talk much more about specific strategies in the next few chapters, but hint, hint: to reprogram the belief, you also have to reprogram the memories and experiences that created it in the first place. Take some time to reflect on these questions as a way to start sorting through some of those "files" that got zipped up into a belief:

- Picture your younger self. What was happening in your life when you first internalized this belief? Who or what influenced it? Can you trace it back to a specific memory, experience, or message you received growing up (try starting with just one belief)?

_____

_____

- Did you observe this belief modeled by your parents, teachers, or society?

_____

- Is this belief still relevant to your life now, or does it feel outdated?

_____

_____

- What prevents you from taking a break, even when you know you need it? What fears come up when you consider slowing down or saying no?

_____

_____

The Belief Inventory: Preserve, Update, and Create

Now that you've identified some of your core limiting beliefs, it's time to take a full inventory. This step involves categorizing beliefs into three groups: **preserve, update, and create**.

1. Preserve

Start with the beliefs that are empowering and serve you well. These are the beliefs you want to preserve and strengthen in your life. Write down the beliefs you want to preserve under this category, and note how you can practice reinforcing them moving forward.

- **Which beliefs do you already hold that make you feel empowered, motivated, and aligned with your goals?**
    -
    -
    -

- **Choose one to focus on from your list. How has this belief positively impacted your mindset or behavior?**

_____

_____

_____

- **What experiences from your life prove this belief is true?**

_____

_____

_____

2. Update

Next, it's time to get super clear on those beliefs that are no longer serving you. These are the limiting beliefs that are keeping you stuck in burnout, stress, or self-doubt. Updating them is not about instantly erasing them, but recognizing that they no longer serve you and gradually reframing your perspective. You'll begin to notice these beliefs as they arise, and over time, you can start to challenge them and reframe your thoughts.

- **Which beliefs are holding you back or causing unnecessary stress (that may no longer fit with who you are and who you want to become)?**
    -
    -
    -

- **Choose one to focus on from your list. How does this belief make you feel?**

_____

_____

- **How would your life be different if that belief didn't have such as grasp on you?**

_____

_____

_____

3. Create

Finally, it's time to create new beliefs that will support you in shifting out of burnout and into a healthier, more balanced mindset. This is where you plant the seeds that will support your growth. These new beliefs may not feel "true" yet, but your brain will start to adapt through practice.

While our built-in negativity bias might want us to prioritize the "negative" beliefs, it's just as important to start thinking about their replacements so that you can begin rewriting that playbook based on your own terms!

- **What are your top 3 values that you want to instill into your life more?**
    -
    -
    -

- **What new beliefs do you want to adopt that would align with those values?**
    -
    -
    -

- **How would your life be different if these beliefs were operating as your "software"?**

_____

_____

_____

- **What small, daily action or experience could you give yourself to reinforce this belief? (Remember, beliefs become "true" through repetition and experience.)**

_____

_____

Now that you've taken an inventory of your beliefs, the next step is to actively work on integrating your chosen beliefs into your daily life. This isn't a one-time exercise—it's an ongoing process that requires practice, awareness, and patience. Your beliefs will evolve as you do.

As you continue through this book, keep revisiting this inventory and remember: reshaping your mindset is a journey. Your beliefs are the foundation of your reality, and by consciously choosing which beliefs to preserve, eliminate, and create, you're taking control of your life in a whole new way. This process will not happen overnight, but every small shift in awareness is a step toward reprogramming your mind to serve you, rather than the other way around.

In the next few chapters, we're going to start diving into specific strategies and habits so that you can begin to integrate those new and updated beliefs into your life, and literally rewire your brain so that your wiring fits with what YOU want, instead of what you were programmed and conditioned for.

Chapter 10

Reprogram: Creating New Coding

"In order to create a different experience, we first need to imagine something new."

We've all heard the saying, *"Change your mind, change your life,"* but let's be real: if it were that easy, this book would've ended several chapters ago. The problem isn't that you're not trying—it's that your brain doesn't *like* change. It's wired for safety and predictability, which means it defaults to what's familiar. Unfortunately, what's familiar might also be keeping you stuck.

You might consciously crave more peace or freedom, but if your brain's been wired for chaos and scarcity for years, it may not even know what peace and freedom feel like anymore. This isn't a failure on your part—it's just how your brain works. Real, lasting change requires more than just wishful thinking or repeating affirmations into the void. You have to get your brain to *actually believe* what you're telling it.

This is why **conscious focus** and **repetition** are so crucial. To reprogram your mind and create a new experience, you have to consistently redirect it toward the thoughts, beliefs, and feelings you *want* to nurture. Without giving your brain a clear alternative, it's like handing it a blank map and saying, *"Good luck!"* It'll just revert to the same old, well-worn roads. Just as those old highways of your mind were built through repeated travel, your new neural pathways need consistent use to become the new default. Think of it like going to the gym: one workout doesn't transform your body. It's the regular, consistent repetition that builds strength. In the same way, new beliefs need constant reinforcement to reshape the brain.

Like a computer, your brain runs on the instructions it's been given—most of which were shaped by years of conditioning. If you want to upgrade from the burnout-and-scarcity operating system to something that feels more aligned with peace and abundance, you'll need to update the coding. You can't simply imagine your new belief once and expect the brain to adopt it. Simply repeating a new belief—"I am worthy of success, regardless of my accomplishments" —won't be enough if your brain isn't *ready* to believe it. Your mind's internal filter, the one that screens what it deems credible, will call BS. Until your brain starts to see evidence of this new belief, it'll default to the old programming. That's why we have to wire your brain for the new belief *before* it can become your new reality.

As you begin the inner work of stripping away layers upon layers of past conditioning and limiting beliefs that hold you back from a new way of living, it can feel uncomfortable—maybe even like you're losing yourself. After all, you've spent so much time and energy being *this* version of you that it might feel like losing part of your identity. But here's the truth: you're not losing *you.* You're letting go of the parts that were never really you to begin with so that you can begin to foster the version of you that is truly you! While one part of you may feel you're losing yourself, there's another perception for you to consider— that you have to make room for what's meant for you, which might mean parting ways with parts of us that we've held for so long that we convince ourselves that it *is* you.

This vision for your future requires **clarity**. You need to define what this new belief looks like, feels like, and sounds like—so vividly that it becomes an internal compass that your brain can use to course correct those outdated printed *Mapquest* directions. Right now, that desired future might feel as real as unicorns, and that's perfectly okay. For now, give yourself permission to dream a little bigger—to get a bit "delulu" in a way that works *for* you. What matters most right now is starting to prime your brain for what *is* possible. Paint a detailed mental picture of the life you're aiming for—joy, peace, freedom, abundance, all of it—because *you deserve it.*

A quick note, though: these new beliefs will struggle to take root unless we also do the work to reframe and rewire the old, limiting beliefs in the chapters ahead. The reason for this goes back to the concept "the conscious brain is the goal setter, and the subconscious is the goal getter." To get them working together, we first need to clean up the "goal-getting" machinery. But for now, let's focus on defining what you *do* want and giving your "goal setter" a crystal-clear picture to aim for.

Put another way, without new input, you can't expect new output. And this is where manifestation comes in—not as some mystical woo-woo magic, but as a practical tool to help your brain identify opportunities and possibilities that align with your goals.

Just like the beliefs we hold about ourselves and our world today were created from a plethora of different, but similar, experiences, the beliefs we *want* to create will only get created through repeated experience. If the new, positive belief is not yet part of your reality, it's up to you to create experiences, real or imagined (since the brain processes both very similarly), that foster that belief. It's not about "fake it 'til you make it". It's "believe it 'til you achieve it".

You are worthy of living a life that aligns with your authentic self. This work of consciously redirecting your brain toward new patterns isn't just about fixing what's broken—it's about creating a life you're excited to wake up to. So, let's dive into the work of conscious creation. You've got this!

Manifestation Without the Woo

When I talk about manifestation, I'm not suggesting you can sit on your couch, chant *"I want a Ferrari,"* and expect it to appear in your driveway (though if that works, please call me). I'm sticking to neuroscience, and less on the "woo". Manifestation isn't about magically thinking your way to success—it's about intentionally priming your brain for new possibilities. In order to understand what "manifestation" really means, there's a few important principles to understand about the brain science of creating. I call it **SPIRMM**. Sure, maybe you have some inappropriate associations to how you just read that, but at least you'll remember it! Let's explore what it stands for:

> **Specific**
> **Positive**
> **Imagination &**
> **Reality**
> **Matching &**
> **Mirroring**

S: Specific

Let's say that you have a dream of having more financial freedom. You may say to yourself, *"I want more money."* Later that day, you're taking a walk outside, and find a penny on the ground. Did you get what you wanted? Probably not! Your brain, however, doesn't know how to read your mind. It works based on a *specific* set of directions.

Remember, your **conscious brain is the goal setter, and the subconscious mind is the goal getter.** So when you settle for an over-generalized goal of more money, that filtering system of your mind will seek out evidence to make that true. If you're not specific enough, however, you may end up disappointed. So get **specific**!

Ask yourself *why* five times to get to the core of your goal:

- Why do I want more money? (To travel.)
- Why do I want to travel? (To feel free.)
- Why do I want to feel free? (To escape daily stress.)

By the fifth "why," you'll likely land on a specific emotional desire. This clarity allows you to give your brain precise input—freedom, peace, or security—so it knows what to filter for.

After you've identified exactly what it is that you want, it's time to start creating a mental movie of exactly what your life would be like. This is where you give yourself full permission to get delusional! Don't just imagine what your life would look like, but involve **all** of your senses. Neurons that fire together, wire together. What would be the sights, sounds, smells, emotions, and even taste of your new future life?

P: Positive

Let's try a quick experiment. After reading this sentence, close your eyes, and whatever you do, ***don't*** think about a big purple elephant! Ok, go for it!

What happened? You likely pictured some sort of representation of a big purple elephant! The reason for this ties back to the language of the mind. The subconscious mind doesn't speak in words and language. It speaks images, metaphors, and emotions. Most importantly, it does not understand the concept of "no" or "not". When we say to ourselves, "I ***don't*** want to be this exhausted and stressed", your mind interprets this as the general concept you're talking about...*stress!*

This also goes back to that negativity bias we talked about before. You're naturally wired to focus more on the negative than the positive. As humans, we're so used to thinking about what we *don't* want, that our brains never have ample opportunity to actually focus on what we *do* want. If we're not aware of our own thoughts and words, that negativity bias will always win, by default.

Even if you do catch yourself thinking or talking about what you don't have, simply switch it up, and reframe it in the affirmative.

I/R: Imagination vs. Reality

Let's try another quick experiment. After reading this, close your eyes and picture the front door to your childhood home. Imagine what it looks like, what sounds you hear when you open it, what you smell when you walk inside, and what emotions come up for you. Try it out!

Did you notice that even though you weren't "there", you were able to remember all of those sensory experiences just as vividly as if you *were* there? This is because your brain can't distinguish between vividly **imagined** experiences and **reality**. When you visualize something, you're activating the same neural pathways as if you were living it.

This is why visualization is such a powerful tool for creation—it allows you to "prime" your brain for new experiences as if they're already happening. This helps your brain to notice opportunities that align with your goals. It's like the example of buying a new car and suddenly seeing that same model everywhere. Those cars were always there; your brain was just using a different algorithm.

This is key to understanding the actual foundations of "manifestation". You're not manifesting a thing. You're manifesting *information*. The data that gets filtered into your conscious brain to make meaning of is simply data until it becomes "in formation". The moment your brain makes meaning of the data, you now have information that you then use that influences your next thoughts, words, and actions.

INFORMATION = Data In Formation

Every time you visualize a desired outcome—whether it's staying calm in stressful situations or feeling confident in a new role—you're essentially rehearsing for reality and priming your brain to filter the information required to make that imagined reality a *real* reality. Pilots do this all the time with flight simulators. Think of visualization as your **life simulator**. It's a rehearsal that strengthens the neural connections tied to your desired reality, making those connections easier to access in real life.

M/M: Matching & Mirroring

It's time for another tough truth: **You cannot create a reality that your brain is not wired to perceive.** You can have a goal. Goals are great. But if your brain is not wired to be able to achieve that goal, you're going to be met with a lot of resistance. Why? Because, you *cannot experience a reality that your brain is not wired to be able to perceive*!

A bee doesn't see humans like we expect them to see us. They see us as a bunch of tiny dots arranged in a honeycomb. They don't see us as we see them because their brains aren't wired in a way to perceive us as we do them. In the same way, your brain is wired for the reality that you perceive right *now*. The *real* reality of the world is the same for a bee or a human, but how we perceive it is based on how our brain is *wired* to perceive it. It's not the objective world that changes, but how we perceive and interpret it that influences what we call our "reality".

In that same line of thinking, our thoughts and the perceptions that come out of those thoughts are highly influenced by our emotions. You *can't* consciously create when your nervous system is screaming, *"RUN",* because the energy required for conscious creation is sucked dry by your body's physiological response to potential or real threat.

For your brain to fully embrace new beliefs, it's not just about thinking differently—you need to *feel* differently, too. This is where **matching and mirroring** come into play. If your desired belief is "I am calm and capable of creating a life of peace," but your emotional state is still one of stress and overwhelm, there's a disconnect. The brain gets confused because your internal state isn't matching the new belief you're trying to program, so the mind and body are at odds with each other.

In other words, your internal state must be a match for your external goal. This is why it's so important to start with the desired **emotion** over anything else. You might not be able to have the "thing" right now, but it's much easier to create the desired emotion. Once your inner state is more peaceful, positive, and intentional, that filtering system (or algorithm of your mind) begins to shift, bringing in a new set of data and information that you can base your next thoughts and actions on. This might feel like a real challenge right now. That's perfectly okay, and to be expected, but we can at least start front-loading with the intention, so that we have a new internal compass when we begin stripping away all of the old, outdated program.

Regulation is key here. By doing more things that shift your nervous system into a calm, regulated state, you create an internal environment that supports the new belief. This allows your brain to access higher cognitive functions—like creativity, problem-solving, and calm decision-making—rather than staying stuck in survival mode. It's a feedback loop: the more you regulate your nervous system, the easier it becomes to access and reinforce the new belief. The more you reinforce the new belief, the more your internal state shifts to match it. And the more those two align, the faster the reprogramming happens.

So get out your pen and journal. Let's put **SPIRMM** into action

1. **What's a SPECIFIC goal that you have? Ask *why* five times.**

_____

_____

2. **Shift any negative language to POSITIVE. Rewrite any "don't want" thoughts into "do want" statements.**

_____

_____

3. **Create a mental movie of your future self already having this goal. Let your IMAGINATION run wild so that you prime your brain for that desired REALITY. As you create this "future-self simulation", be sure to involve as many senses as possible with your visualization.**
   - What does it look like? Sound like? Feel like? Smell/taste like?

_____

_____

_____

4. **How can you practice MATCHING and MIRRORING to create the emotional state tied to your goal today? What's the desired**

emotion and what's something you could do today to foster that feeling?

_____

_____

As you stay consistent with these practices, your brain begins to interpret incoming stimuli with more and more of a bias toward the future self you've been visualizing and the associated empowering beliefs you want to create. This shifts your emotional responses and mindset from survival mode to growth mode. The repetition of imagining and acting from your future self strengthens neural pathways that support success, peace, and resilience. By taking action based on the positive future you've simulated, you reinforce this new mindset through evidence to support that belief, and over time, it becomes more and more part of your default way of thinking.

At the core of all this is the concept we touched on earlier: the brain as a living computer. Its default mode is to run the programs it's been given—your subconscious beliefs. But here's the empowering part: *you* are the programmer. By consciously directing your focus, engaging in visualization, and repeatedly reinforcing new beliefs, you're essentially writing new code for your mind.

Don't be surprised if you begin to notice random synchronicities as you get better and better at this. You may end up finding yourself in an interaction, or presented with an opportunity, that sets you up for that next step toward your future self. You can choose to call it a simple synchronicity, or you can choose to celebrate each and every mini milestone because you know that your brain is slowly but surely rewiring itself to fit with the reality you desire and deserve instead of the one you've been previously wired for.

Practical Strategies for Conscious Creation:

1. Future Self-Simulation Visualization

- **Identify the belief you want to create.** Start by getting clear on what belief will support the future you want to live. Maybe it's "I am resilient" or "I can handle challenges without burning out."
- **Prime your brain through visualization.** Close your eyes and imagine yourself living out this new belief in vivid detail. What are you doing? How are you feeling? The more specific, the better. Engage all your senses.
- **Match your internal state to your belief.** As you visualize, notice your body. Are you tense? Relax your muscles, take a deep breath, and bring your physical state into alignment with the calm, empowered feeling of your new belief.
- **Repeat daily.** This is where repetition comes in. Just like going to the gym, this practice needs consistency. The more you focus on your new belief, the stronger that neural pathway becomes.

2. "What Would Future Self Do?"

Remember those plastic bracelets from back in the 90s for "WWJD" (What Would Jesus Do)? It was like a constant reminder to be on your best behavior and be kind. Similarly, if you're not even sure what your next move should be, you can, instead, think about what that future version of yourself would do. In other words "WWFSD" (what would future self do). If you still can't think of anything, you could also consider what someone else would do that already has what you want. One way to stay aligned with your future self is to **use the mindset of a mentor.** Mentors often represent qualities we admire and strive for. Whenever you're faced with a challenge or decision, pause and ask yourself, *"What would my mentor do in this situation?"* Just be careful that you don't fall into imposter syndrome here. You are unique, and so is your future self!

3. Creating Affirmations that Work

The tricky thing about affirmations is that they require a LOT of effort and repetition, especially if they go against all of your subconscious programming. Think about it. I could tell myself over and over again that *"I am worthy of rest and relaxation"*, but if I still have a subconscious belief that says "rest is lazy", your hardware is going to throw an error message because it can't process that with your current wiring.

This goes back to that 5% vs. 95% rule of the conscious vs. the subconscious mind. You can tell yourself something over and over again consciously, but that's only 5% of the input. So instead of trying to "fake it 'til you make it", I like to take the much more sustainable approach of "work on believing it until you're achieving it." If your subconscious mind doesn't think of it as 100% true that you're worthy of rest and relaxation, then perhaps we just need to revise that affirmation to something like *"I'm working toward being worthy of rest and relaxation."* Much more believable for your subconscious mind, right? Try it out below. Think about 3-5 affirmations that you would like to be true for you in the future. Then, do whatever revising is necessary to make the affirmation believable to your mind as it stands today.

A few helpful sentence stems to get you started:

- I'm working toward...

_____

_____

- I'm becoming more and more...

_____

_____

- I'm creating more...

_____

_____

Chapter 11

Reprogram: Preserving Positive Programs

"The best present you can gift yourself is being present."

We've already explored the beliefs you want to create from scratch, but what about the ones you want to keep? While there's undoubtedly a laundry list of beliefs from your conditioning that need to be shown the exit or rebuilt entirely, there are likely some gems in there, too—beliefs that have actually served you well! No matter how long or short your list of positive beliefs is, these beliefs are incredible tools you already have at your disposal right now! All they need is a little care and reinforcement to keep playing their part.

This chapter is about identifying those helpful beliefs and actively **preserving** them—not just in your thoughts, but in the very neural wiring of your brain. By understanding how to strengthen and protect these positive programs, you can ensure they continue supporting you in living a life that feels aligned, fulfilling, and burnout-resistant.

Oil for the Good

Beliefs are sticky. Unfortunately, the negative ones tend to cling to your brain like superglue, while the positive ones slip away like oil on water. We can blame this on your brain's *negativity bias*—a survival mechanism that prioritizes negative emotional memories, while positive experiences can float by, barely leaving a trace. While this is great for dodging predators back in the day, it's less helpful when you're trying to hold onto beliefs that empower you.

To counteract this negativity bias, we need to consciously work to "soak in the good" by extending the time we focus on positive emotions, thoughts, and experiences. Why? Because **the brain encodes information better when there's a strong emotional component**. Just like your brain remembers past trauma when you're triggered by stress, it also remembers past glimmers when triggered by joy. The longer and more frequently you hold onto and remember these positive experiences, the more neurons fire off in tandem, and when you do this over time, you begin to train your brain to make this way more and more part of your neural wiring.

The key to soaking in the good? Don't just let good moments pass you by. Absorb them, savor them, and let them stick. Your brain—and your future self—will thank you for it.

Matching and Mirroring the Positive

Remember our trusty SPIRMM acronym? This is where **matching and mirroring** comes into play. To create your desired future, you need to align with the emotional and mental state of "future you" that is already living it. Essentially, you're borrowing the feelings and attitudes of your ideal self and mirroring them in the present.

If future-you is calm, successful, and free, start embodying those emotions *right now*—even if it feels unfamiliar or, let's be honest, a little "fake." Your brain doesn't know the difference between what's real and imagined. It just processes the inputs it's experiencing. So, the question becomes: **how do we**

create a more positive internal state when our current external reality isn't exactly rolling out the red carpet for joy?

Let's start here. Think about the last time you felt genuinely calm, happy, or content. Maybe it was during a peaceful morning walk, a deep conversation with a friend, or a moment of solitude sipping your favorite coffee. Now ask yourself: *what did you do with that experience?* Did you savor it, letting it linger and soak into your mind, or did it vanish into the chaos of the next task your brain decided was more important?

Just as imagining or experiencing something activates your neural networks, so does **remembering** it. "Soaking in the good" isn't limited to present-moment experiences. It's also about **revisiting those moments**—especially when you need a spark to reignite the neural wiring connected to your positive beliefs. Think of it as nudging your "algorithm" with a gentle reminder: *"Hey, don't forget this core belief—it's worth prioritizing."*

Gifting (and Regifting) Yourself with Emotional Experiences

Preserving empowering beliefs also means preserving the **emotional experiences** that support them. This means regularly feeding your brain moments of joy, gratitude, pride, and peace. It's not about ignoring the negative or faking perfection; it's about helping your brain recognize that *positive experiences matter, too.*

One of my favorite mindset techniques for this is called **anchoring.** Anchoring is the process of associating specific stimuli—like a touch, word, or even a smell—with a desired emotional state. By doing this, you can essentially trigger that emotional state whenever you need it, giving you an instant reset.

Anchoring engages your brain's filtering system. Repeatedly triggering a peaceful or empowering state through an anchor essentially trains your brain to filter your environment for stimuli that align with that inner state. Over time, this amplifies your awareness of calmness, confidence, or joy and makes it easier to sustain those feelings. When you begin to make this a consistent habit, you're essentially flipping the algorithm on your living, breathing computer (a.k.a. your brain) so it serves you instead of sabotaging you.

Anchoring can happen *during* an experience, like consciously associating a peaceful hike with a moment of peace. Or, it can occur *after the fact,* by reflecting on and mentally connecting an anchor to a past experience. Ideally, though, you'll practice **both**.

Emotional Anchoring in the Moment & After

Imagine this: you're on a peaceful hike, soaking in the beauty of nature. Suddenly, you stumble upon the most stunning waterfall cascading into a pool, with a rainbow shimmering in the mist. Goosebumps rise on your arms as a profound sense of peace and exhilaration washes over you. Then...you simply move on with your hike.

That, my friend, is a **non-example** of anchoring.

Anchoring in the moment, on the other hand, is like pressing "pause" on time and fully immersing yourself in the experience. It's about actively engaging every sense, making the moment more vivid and meaningful to your brain.

Picture this: instead of breezing past the waterfall, you stop. You take it all in:

- The brilliant colors of the rainbow dancing in the mist.
- The cool, refreshing spray of water on your face.
- The earthy, dewy scent of the air.
- The crashing sound of water hitting the rocks below.
- And yes, the taste of that chocolate bar you brought along for the hike.

Most importantly, you focus on how this moment **feels**. Peace. Awe. Joy. Gratitude. You breathe deeply, allowing those emotions to expand within you, imprinting the experience on your brain. You've now gifted yourself a fully immersive, multi-sensory emotional experience.

But that's not all. If you pair this experience with a **positive belief you want to preserve**, like *"I am worthy of peace and calm,"* you've also just provided a crap ton of evidence for your brain to see that belief as true, and continue using that "software" that influences the "algorithm" that determines the probability of what comes next!

Now, you could stop there and move on with your life, and never think about that memory again, but that would be the equivalent of skiing down the slope known as the wiring of your brain one time. One experience alone doesn't carve a deep neural pathway. If, however, we **remember to remember** those positive experiences, and leverage the powerful fact about your brain that it processes remembered events and experienced events in a similar way, you can carve a deeper path. You can solidify the wiring in your brain associated with that memory, emotion, and belief!

Even after a positive emotional experience, **anchoring after the fact** can be just as powerful. Let's say, it's a week later. You're at work. Your inbox is overflowing. You have 10,000 things on your to-do list. You are ***STRESSED***! There's nothing happening around you to make you feel an ounce of calm. Then, you remember that you just need to remember.

You pause, take a few deep breaths, close your eyes, and hit "play" on the mental movie of that moment at the waterfall. You vividly recall every sensory detail, re-immersing yourself in the sights, sounds, smells, and feelings. Your brain processes this remembered event just like it would if you were there, firing off the same neural networks and reinforcing the calm, peaceful state you experienced before. While your brain might want to wander and focus on something else, you continue to bring it back to that memory, regifting yourself the same positive emotional experience.

Will work still continue to be stressful? Probably! The key difference is that this practice helps you **generate the desired inner state from within, regardless of what's happening externally.** And this doesn't just work to feel more calm. It can work for any desired emotion. You want to feel more confident in a particular situation? Take a moment to remember a time from your past where you *did* feel more confident. Perhaps a time when you nailed a presentation or crushed your goals. Replay that memory and soak it in as much as you possibly can, focusing on fostering that inner state. As long as you know how you want to feel, you can leverage the power of your mind to foster that from the inside out. So, find those moments of happiness, big or small, hold onto them tightly, and let them shape the mental wiring of your best self.

But wait! There's more! Because anchoring can also work the other way around. You can also create that desired state from the outside in with a **physical stimulus** prompt!

Physical Anchoring

Do you ever smell something that just takes you right back to your childhood? For me, it's baked bread. It takes me right back to my grandma's kitchen growing up. She was your typical midwest farmer's wife homemaker, and she loved to bake. Being at grandma's house as a child brought me a sense of peace that I didn't always have at home. So, every time that I smell fresh bread, it takes me right back to those memories and emotions. The same thing might happen to you with a song. Either a song that makes you break down in tears every time, or maybe it's your official millennial hype anthem!

The brain's associations are incredibly powerful, particularly when it comes to sensory processing. These associations happen automatically, but you can also *purposefully* create them. Imagine harnessing that power to intentionally anchor emotions like calm, confidence, or joy to specific sensory stimuli, so they're always accessible—like emotional muscle memory.

Your brain processes sensory input (smells, sounds, sights, touch) alongside emotions to form memories. Later, those same sensory triggers can instantly bring up the associated feelings. Smell apple pie? Boom, you're back at Grandma's. Hear your workout anthem? Instant boss-mode.

The cool thing is, you can program this on purpose! If the smell of apple pie makes you feel at peace, keep an apple pie candle nearby. It doesn't have to be the holiday to justify an apple pie candle, right?! If your favorite vacation spot makes you feel free, set one of your favorite photos as your phone background. If blasting a particular playlist makes you feel unstoppable, have it queued up when you're having a rough day at work. Does a hot lavender bubble bath make you feel like a brand new person? Do it more often! ***You're worth the emotional gift to yourself.***

But let's be real, though—you're not always going to have access to candles, playlists, or spa time. That's where **physical touch anchoring** comes in. The sense of touch is always accessible, and it can be just as powerful at evoking emotions. This is why getting a hug from someone makes you feel loved and all warm and fuzzy (unless you're not a hugs person, of course). That physical sensation has a strong association in your brain to being loved, and puts you into that inner state of being, even if just for a moment.

Physical anchoring links a specific *physical action* or sensation—like a hand on your heart or a pinch of your thumb—with a desired emotional state. It's like muscle memory for emotions. Think of it as creating a shortcut: instead of waiting for calm to find you, you call it up by activating the anchor. Over time, with enough repetition, this physical cue can help trigger the emotional state you want to preserve, even during times of high stress.

Here's what the process of creating and reinforcing a physical touch anchor looks like:

1. Choose a Physical Anchor:

This could be something as simple as giving yourself a hug if you're looking to create more inner peace and calm. It might also be something as simple as gently pinching one of your thumbs. The actual physical stimulus doesn't matter all that much, as long as you're not choosing a physical anchor that's already associated with another emotion. For example, if yo u're looking to create confidence in yourself, you wouldn't choose an anchor like giving yourself a hug if a hug is more associated with calm and love than it is confidence for you. If you're at a loss for what to choose, I always suggest a part of your hand since it's readily accessible.

2. **Recall a Positive Emotional Experience:**

Take a few moments to think back to a time when you felt the way you want to feel right now. Recreate and relive the memory vividly: the sights, sounds, smells, and, most importantly, the feelings. Fully immerse yourself in the memory.

3. **Amplify the Emotion:**

Amplify that emotion as much as you can. If it was peace, hold onto that feeling and multiply it by ten! I'm talking give yourself chills type of amplification. Allow it to fill your mind and body. By re-experiencing the emotion, your brain starts to make it more real in the present moment.

4. **Apply the Physical Anchor:**

At the *peak* of the emotion, apply your chosen anchor. For example, place your hand over your heart or squeeze your thumb. Imagine that applying that physical anchor is like hitting the turbo-boost on the emotion. What you're doing here is pairing the emotional state with the physical action, creating a mind/body connection.

5. **Build the Connection:**

Practice, practice, practice. The more you pair the positive emotion with your anchor, the stronger the connection becomes. Over time, you'll be able to activate that state simply by using the anchor, even in stressful or challenging situations.

With physical anchoring, you're essentially carrying a custom emotional "reset button" with you at all times. Whether you need confidence before a big meeting, peace after a chaotic day, or joy in the middle of the mundane, your anchor becomes a reliable way to shift your inner state.

So, pick an anchor, soak in the nostalgic good times, and start training your brain to create that emotional shortcut. Your future stressed-out self will thank you.

Practical Strategies for Anchoring the Good:

1. Morning Meditations:

Of course, meditation is a great practice for anytime of the day, but there's an added benefit of doing it first thing in the morning. By design, your cortisol levels are naturally highest first thing when you wake up—a handy dandy little feature of human biology to help you get out of bed. But what do most of us do with this built-in wake-up call? We douse it with rocket fuel: checking emails, doom-scrolling, and chugging coffee like we're in a competition with ourselves. Spoiler alert: all of that only amplifies your cortisol surge.

Morning meditations counteract your cortisol spike by anchoring you in a peaceful emotional state. It sets a positive tone for the day, allowing your mind and body to establish a baseline of calm. This foundation helps you face whatever chaos the day throws at you without immediately jumping into fight-or-flight mode.

This could be as simple as a 10-minute part of your morning routine. You can make it as simple or fancy as you'd like. The goal is to start the day by priming your brain with more peace and calm.

Bonus points: Super-boost your meditations with a physical anchor, or sound anchor. As you meditate, use your chosen physical anchor (e.g., placing your hand over your heart), or use a "theta brainwaves" playlist for meditation music. The more senses we can involve in that emotion, the better!

2. Daily Emotional Experience Gifts:

Life has a funny way of throwing curveballs, doesn't it? Between the chaos, the constant stream of bad news, and the stressors that seem to multiply daily, it can feel like you're drowning in negativity. But if we let ourselves fall into the mindset that life is just a series of unfortunate events happening *to* us, we become victims of our own life and miss out on the other perspective: life is happening *for* us.

What I hope you're starting to understand is that we are both active and passive participants in this journey called life. You're both a passenger and a driver, a creator and a reactor. While you'll inevitably react to challenges (because life isn't a walk in the park), you also have the power to create experiences that align with your desired emotional state. In other words, when life around you feels chaotic, that's your opportunity to step up and gift yourself positive emotional experiences. We are simultaneously reacting and creating at the same time.

It's hard to find peace if you don't know what peace feels like. So, start by identifying the emotional state you're craving. If it's difficult to articulate exactly what you want to feel, start with the opposite—what don't you want to feel? Then, flip it. For example, if you feel stressed and overwhelmed, maybe you're craving calm, relaxation, or joy. Once you've pinpointed the emotion, you're halfway there.

Now, think back to moments that made you feel how you want to feel now. It could be something as simple as time spent with loved ones, a particular hobby, or a vacation that brought you peace. Whatever it is, go *do that thing again*. It doesn't matter if it's a walk in nature, a deep conversation, or a cozy day with your favorite book. The point is to intentionally create a moment that brings you back to that emotional state.

"But I don't have the time or energy for that!" I hear you. I've got good news for you, though, that you already know! Your brain can't tell the difference between an actual experience and a vividly imagined memory of an experience. So, even if you can't physically recreate the experience, you can *mentally* go back there. Take a few minutes to replay that moment in your mind, bringing it to life by tapping into all your senses. Picture the sights, sounds, smells—let your brain re-experience the emotions that came with it.

Bonus points: Pair your positive emotional experiences with sensory anchors. For example, when remembering a calming experience, you might place your hand on your heart (physical anchor), or listen to the same playlist you had in the background during the experience (sound anchor). The more senses you involve, the more you'll reinforce the emotional connection.

3. Evening Gratitude Journaling

We've all heard about the power of gratitude, but practicing gratitude journaling at night can have a profound impact on how your brain processes emotions and memories. By focusing on positive experiences before bed, you're doing more than just boosting your mood—you're actively rewiring your brain to notice more of the good in your life. Let's explore the science behind this and how you can supercharge your gratitude practice for lasting change.

Research suggests that the last thoughts we have before sleep have a profound impact on the brain's ability to process and consolidate memories during REM sleep. This phase of sleep is when your brain processes emotional experiences, reinforcing those that hold significance. If the last thing you're doing before bed is stressing yourself out about tomorrow, you are essentially prioritizing the storage of stressful memories first. When you end your day with a focus on gratitude and positive emotions, you prime your brain to process memories related to that same state. By choosing to focus on what went well, what you're thankful for, and moments of joy, you're helping your brain rewire itself for more positivity and peace, even in your sleep.

At the end of every day, start writing down at least 3 things that you're grateful for from the day. Note any moments where you took rest or experienced joy, reinforcing the belief that these moments are valuable. It doesn't have to be anything big or fancy. It's simply the act of shifting your perspective toward gratitude and away from scarcity and fear.

To make your gratitude journaling even more powerful, be sure to focus on the emotion as much or more than the thing. Instead of saying, "I'm grateful for the opportunity to spend the day at the beach", say "I'm grateful for the

peace and calm I received from spending the day at the beach." This is you reinforcing the association of the experience to the emotion, which will make it easier for your brain to make future associations to this same emotion.
Bonus Points: If you're ready to level up your gratitude practice, consider other ways that you might create additional stimulus to anchor yourself to peace, calm, and gratitude. Perhaps it's lighting your favorite candle or playing your favorite relaxation playlist while you do this.

Anchoring is not a quick fix, but over time, it's one of the most effective ways to shift your brain's wiring. Once your brain has preserved those positive beliefs and patterns, they become a foundation you can return to over and over. Preserving the positive is an ongoing process, one that requires consistent effort and attention. The oil may be slipperier than the glue, but with enough practice, you'll find that soaking in the good is not only beneficial in the moment, but also in rewiring your brain for how you want to feel in the future.

Repetition is key—whether you're soaking in the good, using sensory anchors, or engaging in morning meditation, it's about teaching your brain to prioritize these positive experiences. You're not just breaking the cycle—you're building a completely new one, where the automatic responses you've programmed serve your well-being instead of feeding burnout.

Chapter 12

Reprogram: Updating Outdated Software

"The greatest discovery of my generation is that a human being can alter their life by altering their attitudes of mind."

- William James (one of my favorite famous philosopher/psychologists)

By now, you've hopefully gained a deeper understanding of how subconscious beliefs shape your reality. You've identified the beliefs you want to preserve and started dreaming up new ones to create. But without this crucial final step, all the work you've done so far might not be as effective as you'd like. Why? Because lingering beliefs from your past are still lurking in the background, ready to disrupt your journey toward the new path you're creating.

Let's be real—these old, limiting beliefs are the hardest to crack, especially if they've been ingrained since childhood. Why is this so difficult? As we've discussed throughout this book, your brain's number one job is to keep you safe. And those outdated beliefs, no matter how limiting they might be now, once served as protective mechanisms. The brain doesn't want to let go of anything it thinks is essential for your survival. Even if those beliefs are no longer serving you, your brain holds onto them like a software program that hasn't seen an upgrade since Y2K.

Many of those beliefs are outdated, inefficient, and, frankly, holding you back. It's time to hit the reset button and reprogram them. In this chapter, we'll dig into the process of updating these old mental programs, replacing the outdated software with new, healthier beliefs that align with the life you want to create.

Eliminating vs. Upgrading

Our brains are wired for protection, and negative experiences—big or small—often shape the lens through which we see the world. Remember, our stress response isn't just triggered by actual danger; it's often triggered by cues tied to unresolved emotions or limiting beliefs rooted in earlier experiences. These cues—be they sensory (a smell, sound, or image) or cognitive (a thought, word, or situation)—activate neural pathways wired through repetition. If a past experience taught you that asking for support was a sign of weakness, or that taking time to yourself was something to feel guilty about, that becomes the filter for all future experiences. These experiences alter our internal filtering process, changing the "algorithm" of our living, breathing computer. Over time, this creates a reality where we expect danger, disappointment, or failure, even when those things aren't actually present in the situation at hand.

This filtering system is the reason why, even if you logically know that a belief is no longer helpful, your brain still insists on holding on to it. Think of your subconscious as a cautious IT administrator, refusing to uninstall outdated software just in case it's needed someday. If left unchecked, these outdated programs are what can trap you in an endless loop of stress and unhelpful reactions.

Consciously, you may know that certain aspects of the "old program" are no longer serving you. But the subconscious "software" continues to operate on autopilot, regardless of your current conscious thoughts. When you find yourself repeating old patterns or reacting in ways that don't make sense, it's simply your brain executing the programming it has stored. This is the "hardware" (your brain) carrying out the instructions of the "software" (your subconscious beliefs).

This is the part that you have to tackle before you can start creating and "manifesting". Not only do you need to have a new belief to guide you in the direction you want to go, but you also need to reframe how those previous memories and experiences are wired in your brain so that those limiting subconscious beliefs don't sabotage your growth and potential by canceling its possibility!

To break free from this outdated programming, you need to go deep into the software and start rewriting it—not in a way that erases the events of your past, but in a way that allows you to move forward with a new perspective. The key here is not to disregard your feelings or gaslight yourself; it's about learning how to manage your emotional responses so that the stress doesn't spiral out of control. Feeling the emotion is essential; suppressing it is what creates tension, making the stress more intense in the long run. It's about managing the "rock splash" (the intense, immediate stress) and the "ripple effects" (the lasting thought patterns that follow), so that your stress response doesn't keep triggering on repeat.

This isn't about simply eliminating the old trauma and associated beliefs. That would be too risky for your brain, since those beliefs once kept you safe at one point or another. Instead, it's about updating and softening the intensity of those negative memories so that they are filtered through a different belief that is more self-serving.

So, I see this as less about eliminating, and more about just turning down the volume and updating those negative beliefs and associated thoughts when they're *not* needed for our survival. Think about it— if our ancestors were to just completely rewrite the software of "rustle in the bushes is a threat", then there would have been a whole heck of a lot more sabertooth tiger attacks.

The process of updating this "software" isn't always comfortable. It will likely be challenging, and it will take time because it feels like you're stepping away from a safety net. But the good news is that we know it's possible, thanks to neuroplasticity. This is where the tool of **reframing** comes in—a way to reparent your brain with new, updated instructions so that your subconscious patterns align with who you want to be now, rather than who you were in the past.

The Power of Reframing: Updating the Software

In Chapter 9, you spent time identifying the beliefs you're ready to update. The next step is to actively challenge and reframe the experiences that created them in the first place. This means questioning the validity of these past perceptions and replacing them with more empowering alternatives.

Reframing is one of the most powerful tools for shifting out of limiting beliefs because it allows you to change how you interpret and respond to situations and experiences. Essentially, you're allowing your brain the opportunity to filter any new or previous experiences of stress and anxiety through a different algorithm— one that aligns with your new beliefs, rather than the ones that have been running the show beneath the surface all these years. The goal isn't to deny the situation or sugarcoat your feelings, but to consciously choose a perspective that helps, rather than harms.

When you use reframing in stressful situations, you engage your prefrontal cortex—the rational, planning part of your brain. Instead of reacting impulsively or emotionally, you pause, assess the situation from a new angle, and turn down the volume on the emotional charge. This helps prevent your stress response from escalating by neutralizing the emotional charge that would normally add more carbonation to that "shaken up soda bottle".

This process ties back to that filtering system we discussed earlier. Your brain filters out irrelevant information and only allows in what aligns with your current beliefs. When you reframe a situation, you're giving your brain new instructions. You're retraining your brain so your past doesn't continue to dictate your future.

To really solidify this whole idea of reframing, let's revisit that cycle that we discussed before.

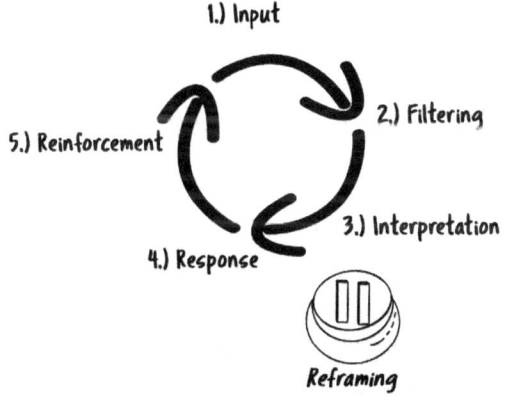

Reframing works by disrupting this cycle between two critical points: **interpretation** and **response**. Instead of allowing your brain to interpret stressors in the same automatic way, through the filter of old, limiting beliefs, reframing helps you pause, reinterpret the situation, and respond from a more useful perspective. You can use reframing in real-time for present situations, or for those past experiences that still carry so much emotional weight. In both cases, reframing helps shift your perspective and response, wiring your brain for healthier, more balanced responses to stress.

Let's revisit one of the most destructive limiting beliefs that tends to haunt the minds of so many millennials— that rest is lazy and must be earned through pushing yourself beyond your limits to be justified. With this belief so deeply ingrained in our subconscious mind, it becomes part of the filtering system for our reality. We may find a moment of peace where we lay down to take a break from the hustle, only for that moment of calm to be interrupted by that old narrative that convinces you that you should be doing something more productive. Now, there you are stressing yourself out about the fact that you're finally able to experience a moment of stress-free bliss!

This limiting belief was solidified through many of those same experiences and shared trauma that we discussed earlier in the book. Keep in mind, beliefs are simply a "zip folder" of a bunch of consolidated, related memories and experiences. This means that, in order to reprogram the belief, we also have to reframe the experiences that created that belief in the first place.

For instance, when you feel that sense of guilt or shame for actually putting yourself first, this is a prime opportunity to shift that narrative, and revise your perspective on past experiences, so that it's filtered through a more self-serving belief. While the automatic reaction may be guilt or inadequacy, you create just enough of a pause to explore another perspective: "Maybe my parents were under stress themselves, and their criticism wasn't about my worth but about their own overwhelm." This new narrative not only reduces the emotional charge of those past memories, but also creates space for a self-serving belief so that those previous experiences are re-filtered in a way that allows you to move forward in a new direction with a sense of internal safety.

As you become more aware of how that limiting belief shows up in your life, you can begin to challenge it by asking, *"Is this really true? What evidence do I have that rest **is** valuable and necessary?"* From there, you can reframe the belief to something more supportive, such as, "Rest is essential for my well-being and productivity, regardless of what I was taught." As you make reframing a habit, you start to update your brain's automatic responses to stress, creating new neural pathways that reinforce beliefs that support your well-being.

This reparenting is both a challenge and an opportunity for growth. Over time, as you practice reframing, this new response becomes wired into your brain's circuitry. The next time a similar situation arises, your brain will be more likely to follow the reframed approach, rather than defaulting to burnout-related behaviors. As an added benefit, you also reduce the intensity of the stress response should that scenario occur in the future, so that you stay more centered and less reactive.

This doesn't happen overnight, though. Just as you spent years reinforcing the neural pathways that support burnout and stress, it will take time to reverse those pathways and create new ones. This is where neuroplasticity comes to save the day once again. With consistent reframing, your brain will begin to create new connections, prioritizing responses that are calmer, more balanced, and less reactive. Over time, your brain will rely less on the old, stress-filled pathways, and more on the healthier, more productive responses you're cultivating.

Practical Strategies for Reframing:

1. Reframe a Recent Stressful Situation:

Imagine this. You're at work and find out your project deadline has been moved up by two days. Immediately, your brain interprets this as a stressor: *"I have to get this done **right now**"* or *"I'm going to mess this up, and my boss will be disappointed, and I'll get fired."* Your amygdala kicks into fight-or-flight mode, and you start to feel the familiar signs of overwhelm, anxiety, and burnout. Before long, you've spent hours in a stressed state, producing subpar work.

But what if you could reframe in that moment? Instead of spiraling into stress, you could consciously choose to reinterpret the deadline change. Your past conditioning might tell you, *"We're already running out of time. This needs to be done ASAP, or I'll fail."* However, you could reframe it by saying, *"If I take a 10-minute break or a short walk, I'll have a much clearer mind to focus on this"* or *"I can use this as an opportunity to prove to myself that giving my body what it needs makes me more productive."* By reframing the situation, you shift the narrative and give your brain new instructions. You're teaching yourself that this doesn't have to be the way you always react.

Now, it's your turn to try this out! Here's the steps:

Reflect on the Initial Interpretation. Write down a recent event that triggered stress or anxiety. Was it a deadline? A difficult conversation? An association to something from your past? Take a deep breath, allow yourself to feel the emotion, and then take a step back from the situation. Describe how you initially interpreted it and what belief was at the core of your response (e.g., "I failed at work, which means I'm not good enough").

Challenge & Reframe the Initial Interpretation. Ask yourself if the initial thought is based on reality or if it's just a result of your subconscious programming. "Where did this come from? Is this belief true for me today?" Does this situation have to be negative (it's ok if it does)? What would happen if you saw it from a different perspective? What alternative perspective could you take? How can you view it as an opportunity for growth or learning?

Try "What If" Scenarios. When a negative belief feels overpowering, try flipping it around with a simple "What if" statement. Instead of *"What if I fail?"* ask yourself, *"What if this is a learning opportunity?"* This simple reframing exercise lets your brain consider possibilities beyond failure and opens up space for new, positive beliefs to take root.

Write a new interpretation that challenges your initial belief and serves the new beliefs you want to create in its place.

2. **Practice Imagery Rescripting for Past Situations:**

As you get better at reframing in real-time, you can also start addressing some of the older memories and experiences that have contributed to your current belief system. This is where **imagery rescripting** comes into play. Imagery rescripting is a technique that allows you to revisit past memories and experiences that may still have a hold on you, but with a twist: you "edit" the script so that it unfolds through the lens of your new, more empowering belief system. *Important note:* This is not meant to completely overwrite any past trauma. If you haven't worked through the emotions first, the reframing part will be much more challenging. You've got to feel, then deal, then heal.

For example, let's say a coworker's comment from the past about your performance triggers feelings of inadequacy. Every time you see or work with that person, you're reminded of the comment and the way it makes you feel. The result might be that you curl up in a ball of stress whenever they're around. By reframing this past memory, you could tell yourself, "I value feedback, but my worth isn't tied to anyone's opinion." As you continue to reinterpret this event from that new perspective, you might notice that you're less and less triggered by that coworker's presence. Or, if you genuinely value their feedback, you could reframe it as an opportunity to grow, while practicing self-compassion.

Here's the play-by-play for reframing past experiences through a new filter:

First, Identify Negative Memories. Think back to a memory that has had a negative impact on your self-esteem or sense of worth. It might be an event where you felt ashamed, scared, or incapable. These memories often carry the weight of your old beliefs about yourself, which were formed by early life experiences or past trauma.

Reframe the Memory from the Present Moment. Revisit this memory, but instead of interpreting it through the lens of your old belief system, try to interpret it through the new, more self-empowering beliefs you are developing.

Ask yourself:

- What did I learn about myself through this experience?
- How does this event fit into the broader narrative of my growth and resilience?
- How can I see this as an opportunity for strength, rather than as a reflection of my inadequacy?

Rescript the Memory. Replay the memory in your mind, but with the script edited. See the events unfolding from a different perspective. For example, if you had a traumatic experience where you felt rejected, you might replay it imagining yourself standing tall and confidently handling the situation, rather than shrinking in fear. If you experienced failure, rescript it as a moment of learning, where you picked yourself up, adjusted, and grew stronger from the experience. This is you taking advantage of the fact that your brain processes real experiences and simulated experiences in your mind in the same way!

Engage All Your Senses: The more vivid and sensory-rich your mental rescripting is, the more powerful the impact on your brain will be. As you revisit the memory from a new lens, imagine the sights, sounds, and even smells of the environment. The more senses you can engage, the more neural networks in your brain will fire, helping to anchor this new perspective into your memory.

Integrate Your New Perspective: Once you've rescripted the memory, let yourself fully experience the new version. How do you feel now? What has changed in your perception of yourself and the situation? Imagine the positive feelings associated with this new interpretation, like empowerment, calm, or pride.

Reimagine Entire Parts of the Memory: As you become more comfortable with this process, you may be able to go even further and rescript entire sections of the memory. This might mean imagining what the experience would have been like if you had known the things you know now—whether that's self-compassion, personal strength, or a deeper understanding of your own worth. For instance, if you've had a difficult conversation in the past that left you feeling defeated, you might replay it as a conversation where you communicate your needs confidently, feeling empowered to set boundaries and advocate for yourself.

3. **The Power of "Yet"**

Let's face it: no matter how hard we try to reframe our thoughts and shift our beliefs, those negative, self-sabotaging thoughts still creep in. Thoughts like "I'm not good enough" or "I'll never get what I want" are often the first to show up when we feel challenged. It's your brain's built-in negativity bias at work, and it's relentless. But these thoughts don't have to define you, and you don't have to beat yourself up for it. In fact, you can start shifting them with the power of just one little word: **Yet.**

Adding "yet" to the end of a negative thought completely changes its energy. It's a subtle but powerful way to remind your brain that just because something isn't true *right now* doesn't mean it won't be true in the future. It leaves the door open for the possibilities of the future in a way that doesn't shut your brain off to that algorithm. When your brain sees the word "yet," it becomes alert to opportunities, evidence, and experiences that support the idea of future change. Your brain will start seeking out proof that you're capable of transformation.

For example:

- Instead of saying, "*I'm not experienced enough*," say, "*I'm not experienced enough **yet**.*"
- Instead of "*I'll never be at peace*," try "*I'm not at peace **yet**.*"

One of my favorite stories that exemplifies the power of "yet" is the story of Roger Bannister. Before 1954, the scientific and health community were all in agreement that it was impossible to run a mile under 4 minutes. If anyone tried, they believed that their heart would basically explode. Roger Bannister, however, was a man that lived for the "yet". In May of 1954, Bannister became the first person to run a mile in under 4 minutes— 3 minutes and 59.4 seconds to be precise. Since then, that record has gone on to be broken several times, with the fastest mile today being 3 minutes and 43 seconds. Bannister didn't just shatter a record. He shattered a belief.

If there's one word in the English language that represents the emotional charge of hope and possibility, it's **"yet"**.

The work of reframing your experiences and limiting beliefs is a process that requires patience and commitment. But every time you choose to reframe a negative belief or automatic response, you're actively reprogramming your subconscious. It may feel uncomfortable at first because you're rewriting your brain's algorithm to prioritize positive, growth-focused beliefs rather than defaulting to protection-mode patterns. The investment that you're making in this journey of reparenting is what is going to allow you to shift from "just surviving" to thriving, supporting a reality where you're no longer defined by your past, and begin breaking out of the mindset that's no longer serving you, and creating space for a healthier, more sustainable way of living. You're out here building your new FYP of life brick by brick!

Part 4:
REDISCOVER

Chapter 13

Rediscover: Finding vs. Rediscovering

"When you find yourself cocooning in darkness and isolation, remember that this is the same place where caterpillars go to become butterflies."

I've never much liked the concept of "finding yourself." Find myself? I'm right here! What exactly am I supposed to be searching for? For years, especially in my late 20s and early 30s, I tried desperately to "find myself."

What I've come to realize, however, is that there was nothing to find. Instead of *finding yourself*, maybe we should think about it as **rediscovering** yourself.

The truth is, you've always been you. The truest, most authentic version of yourself? It's still there, patiently waiting. It's just been buried under layers of conditioning, societal expectations, and the endless "shoulds" that have crowded out the person you were before the world told you who to be. For so long, you had to prioritize everyone and everything except yourself. In the process, perhaps you lost touch with the most authentic essence of who you are.

During my own healing journey, I came across a social media post about the top regrets of people on their deathbeds (I know, kind of dark). The top regret, by far, was: *"I wish I'd had the courage to live a life more true to myself, not the life others expected of me."* For me, this is a constant reminder that life is short, and we either let it happen to us or we make it happen for us.

It was around that same time when I started asking myself the really big, audacious questions: Whose goals was I chasing? Were they truly mine, or just the ones society and others had imposed on me? What else is there beyond the 9-to-5 grind, just trying to survive? And could I really keep going like this for the next 30 years until, with any luck, I could retire?!

I had enough evidence that the old way of doing things no longer worked. But what now? If the old way wasn't working, then what was the replacement? And perhaps the most audacious question of all: *What would I do if I valued myself above anyone or anything else?*

I wanted nothing more than for that to be true for me. But after years of doing things the same way, anything else felt like stepping into the great unknown—terrifying, uncomfortable, and exhausting. It felt safer to keep "masking up," pretending I was okay, and going through the motions, rather than muster the energy to chase new passions or set new intentions. My desire for creativity and purpose had been stifled by fear and stress.

But I wasn't willing to let that rule my life anymore. I knew I couldn't keep going this way forever, constantly running on empty while the rules kept changing and the goalposts kept moving. As I was doing the inner work of reprogramming my mind and reframing my life, it hit me: maybe it *wasn't* that I wasn't successful. Maybe I just needed to redefine what success actually meant—to *me*. What if success meant simply being myself, without trying to meet everyone else's standards and expectations? What if I started living for my own dreams and goals, rather than those handed to me? And most importantly, what if *who I am is enough*? Period. No conditions attached.

This isn't about some grand scheme where you'll be living some dream life with all the materialistic things we so often strive for as humans. I'm not here to dictate what your dreams and future intentions are. That's for you to decide. This is about giving yourself the permission, and creating enough internal safety so that you start living out your life as you'd like, *whatever* that looks like of you. Once your brain (goal setter) and your mind (goal getter) are on the same page, the possibilities become limitless!

This brings us to where you are now: **Rediscover**. The groundwork you've already laid—through self-awareness, regulating your nervous system, and reprogramming subconscious beliefs—has brought you here. This is the phase where all your inner work starts to show tangible, meaningful results. You've already begun the process of hacking outdated programming, rewiring old patterns, and creating a safe internal space where healing can unfold naturally.

The best part? This rediscovery process isn't about forcing change or striving for it. It's about allowing it. Like clearing years of fog from a mirror, you're coming back to the very essence of who you've always been—once everything else is stripped away and you feel safe enough to drop the shields and masks.

This journey has not only prepared your brain to feel safe enough to reconnect with your authentic self, but it has also reconditioned your mind and nervous system to welcome growth, change, and connection with less resistance. This is where your powerful, intentional brain comes back online, like a laser that's been dimmed for too long. You've done the inner work to create enough safety from the inside out, so that your light can finally shine again.

This is the stage where you begin to fulfill your need for validation more internally than externally. You'll start making decisions based on your authenticity, not your conditioning. This phase isn't just about becoming unstuck—it's about returning to a version of yourself that's unburdened by old labels and societal expectations. As you shed those conditioned beliefs and outdated programming, new perspectives, strengths, and emotions will naturally emerge. It's exhilarating—but also challenging.

Remember the quiet metamorphosis of a caterpillar turning into a butterfly I mentioned in the beginning of the book? It's a process that happens naturally, almost imperceptibly, but its effects are profound and permanent. This final stage of the journey—at least this part of it—is about allowing your transformation to unfold in the same way. As you emerge into the person you've always been, you'll not only be rewiring your mindset—you'll be rediscovering the authentic self that burnout and survival mode once buried.

Along the way, expect both incredible shifts and tough reckonings. This journey isn't always easy. Old wounds may resurface, and at times, you might feel like you're moving backward. But these moments? They're proof of progress. They mean your brain feels safe enough to revisit and release what's been buried. You've created the internal safety necessary for this healing to happen—a sign that you're on the other side of the hardest part.

Just as a butterfly doesn't need to strive to become a butterfly, you won't need to force this new stage of life. It will happen organically as your brain, body, and mind recalibrate to your new beliefs and worldview. You may rediscover a renewed sense of curiosity, authentic confidence, and deeper, more meaningful relationships. You'll experience new levels of self-trust and resilience, and perhaps most importantly, you'll embrace the idea that you are, and always have been, **enough**.

To prime yourself for the changes and anticipated growth ahead, I've consolidated this process down to ten aspects of your rediscovery that you can get excited about—and the **"watch-out-fors"** so that you're prepared for potential setbacks. This list isn't exhaustive, but it's a solid starting point as you continue down this path less taken. These milestones are signals that your truest self is emerging and your wings are unfolding. A reminder that you're exactly where you're meant to be.

1. Deepened Sense of Self-Acceptance

What to Get Excited About: As you peel back the layers of who you *thought* you needed to be in order to gain acceptance, you'll uncover a core self rooted in authenticity, self-compassion, and self-acceptance. This newfound self-acceptance brings more freedom from perfectionism, the exhausting pursuit of external validation, and the societal "shoulds" that used to drive you. You'll begin to see your quirks, flaws, and strengths as uniquely you. It's like finally removing an uncomfortable mask you've worn for years. You start to see yourself not as broken, but as human. You'll notice you have more patience and understanding for yourself, and as a result, you'll likely see your relationships with others and yourself flourish in unexpected ways.

What to Be Prepared For: Self-acceptance doesn't happen overnight, and, ironically, as you get closer to your authentic self, you may notice an initial increase in self-doubt or discomfort. This is a natural response to change, as the mind isn't always eager to release its old, familiar beliefs about who you should be. As familiar, conditioned beliefs about yourself begin to dissolve, it may feel a bit disorienting at first. It may trigger thoughts like, *"Who am I now if I'm not always striving for perfection?"* or *"Is this okay?"* Understand that this is part of the process. Lean into the discomfort—it's a sign that you're breaking free from old patterns and embracing a truer, more complete version of yourself. Remember, this isn't about becoming someone new—it's about rediscovering the essence of who you've always been, just beneath the surface of your old conditioning.

2. Reawakened Inner Confidence

What to Get Excited About: As you shed conditioned beliefs and embrace your authentic self, a powerful confidence begins to emerge. But this isn't the kind of confidence that relies on external validation, achievements, or outsourcing your worth. It's the quiet, grounded assurance that comes from truly trusting yourself. This confidence is about truly knowing who you are, what you stand for, and recognizing your unique strengths and worth. With it, you'll find yourself less inclined to overthink decisions or seek permission to take up space. You'll feel emboldened to pursue goals with courage, adapt to challenges without fearing failure, and stop second-guessing your abilities. It's not about being fearless—it's about knowing that, no matter what, you'll figure it out. You may find yourself stepping into opportunities you once hesitated to pursue, speaking up with conviction, or simply feeling more at ease in your own skin. Think of it as shifting from "I hope I can" to "I know I will."

What to Be Prepared For: Newfound confidence might feel alien, even threatening, to the parts of you used to playing small. Reawakening inner confidence can be accompanied by moments of self-doubt, especially as you let go of familiar but limiting beliefs. Sometimes, this new confidence might feel unfamiliar. You may worry about coming across as "too much". People who are accustomed to your previous patterns, especially those who benefited from your self-doubt, might even react differently to this newfound self-assuredness. These feelings are natural and part of the process, and they serve as reminders that confidence, like any skill, strengthens over time. Think of these growing pains as temporary and necessary—they're simply part of the process. The reward is a sense of inner security that no one can take away. With each step, you'll grow into a version of yourself that's secure, self-assured, and unapologetically authentic.

3. Emotional Clarity and Awareness

What to Get Excited About: Rediscovering yourself comes with a renewed, vibrant awareness of your emotional landscape. With a regulated nervous system and a decluttered mind, you'll begin to recognize your emotions with greater precision, understanding their origins and what they're trying to communicate. This clarity means you'll be able to respond to emotions intentionally rather than reacting impulsively. You'll begin to notice when your body signals rest or connection—and trust yourself to honor it. This heightened emotional awareness transforms emotions from chaotic forces into helpful allies that guide your decisions, creativity, and relationships. It's like upgrading your emotional software—less lag, more intuitive processing.

What to Be Prepared For: With this enhanced emotional clarity, old emotions, and even unresolved traumas, may rise to the surface. As your nervous system becomes more regulated and your mind decluttered, your brain will recognize that it's now safe enough to process these stored emotions. It's like when someone who has been in a serious accident wakes up with no memory of the event—sometimes, the brain stores trauma in the subconscious until it feels you're safe enough to deal with it. Picture it like unclogging a drain—the water may back up before it can flow freely again. While this can be uncomfortable, it's an opportunity for healing, not an emotional setback. Thanks to the internal safety you've created, these emotional surges can be processed constructively, rather than feeling overwhelming. You might find yourself feeling more raw or more sensitive than usual. Be patient with yourself as you navigate through this murkiness, and give yourself grace. Processing these resurfaced emotions might feel tough initially, but remember, this is the path to healing and release, which will ultimately allow you to move forward unburdened.

4. Clarity on Personal Values and Priorities

What to Get Excited About: With a clearer mind and greater alignment to your authentic self, you'll start to see your personal values and priorities with renewed, much sharper focus. This clarity can simplify decision-making, helping you align your life with what truly matters. Decisions that once felt overwhelming will now feel intuitive because they align with what truly matters to you. It's less about having a five-year plan and more about reconnecting with the intentions of joy, purpose, and play. Your definition of things like happiness and success may drastically shift. This shift should amplify the newfound sense of peace in your life, knowing that you're investing your time, energy, and heart into things that genuinely resonate with who you are. Many people describe this as feeling "centered" or "anchored" in their lives, unshaken by distractions or external pressures. You'll notice a shift from chasing external metrics of success to living in alignment with your own internal compass.

What to Be Prepared For: With this newfound clarity, you may face difficult realizations, especially when it reveals areas of misalignment in your life—whether in relationships, work, or habits that no longer serve you. You might feel a strong desire to quit your job and travel the world, but you also know that you probably can't afford to do that (at least long term). While you may know exactly what you value, you might also find it difficult to bring those values to life in your daily routines. Realigning your life with your authentic values may require some uncomfortable shifts, but these shifts don't have to be monumental. You may realize that certain aspects of your life need to change for you to feel aligned. These realizations can feel daunting, but are necessary for creating space for what aligns with your values. Be gentle with yourself as you assess these areas. Don't forget that change doesn't have to happen overnight. Give yourself permission to move at your own pace when it comes to course correcting any misalignments.

5. Reconnection with Joy and Curiosity

What to Get Excited About: Rediscovery often comes with a childlike sense of wonder and excitement for life's simple pleasures. Burnout numbs us to joy and curiosity, but uncovering your true self reignites them. As you reconnect with yourself, you'll find that joy and curiosity return in unexpected ways. You may find yourself drawn to playful, creative, or adventurous pursuits you may have dismissed as frivolous. This might mean rediscovering old hobbies, enjoying new experiences, or simply finding contentment in the moments between the moments. This "soaking in the good" makes everyday experiences feel richer and more meaningful, while this renewed curiosity enhances your appreciation for life's simple pleasures. Get ready for your world to feel much more alive!

What to Be Prepared For: After periods of burnout, allowing yourself to fully embrace joy and curiosity may feel vulnerable or even strange. You may experience an initial reluctance to fully embrace these feelings, as old beliefs about whether you "deserve" joy resurface. You may also feel pulled back into old ways of thinking where you spend those moments of peace catastrophizing about what next bad thing might be around the corner. These thoughts and future-based predictions are remnants of past conditioning and trauma, and as you continue this work, you'll gradually feel safer and more open to experiencing joy without as much resistance and reservation. The more you lean into joy, *without second-guessing your right to feel it*, the easier it becomes to trust it.

6. Increased Sense of Inner Peace and Calm

What to Get Excited About: As you align more and more with your authentic self, a natural sense of peace and calm follows. The noise of old worries, doubts, and mental chatter fades as you develop the skills to self-regulate and reframe. This peace is not just internal—it also manifests physically, with better sleep and an overall sense of well-being. It allows you to approach challenges from a place of balance, maintaining your center amidst life's inevitable ups and downs. Old patterns that once triggered panic will no longer rattle you because you've built tools and resilience to navigate them. You'll realize that stress and chaos are inevitable parts of life, but so are the moments of peace and calm you've cultivated. From this new balanced perspective, you'll be able to finally rest without spiraling into guilt and shame!

What to Be Prepared For: Peace doesn't mean immunity to stress—it's about resilience to stress. Initially, this calm might feel fragile or fleeting, as those same old triggers will always be there waiting to test your progress. You may wonder if this calm is sustainable, or question its authenticity. Expect setbacks but recognize them as opportunities to apply your new tools. This, again, is simply part of the journey, where inner peace becomes a steady undercurrent, even if life's storms occasionally disrupt it (which they will). Life won't be all rainbows and butterflies, but you'll have built a consistent inner state of greater peace that allows you to confront stress in new ways that don't keep you stuck there as long.

7. Natural Strengthening of Boundaries

What to Get Excited About: Rediscovering yourself and your inherent worth naturally leads to a deeper understanding of and respect for your boundaries. Recognizing your worth allows you to honor your energy and time more intentionally. Without as much urgency, self-induced pressure, or people-pleasing tendencies, you'll feel more empowered to set limits that honor your energy and well-being. You'll feel more comfortable saying "no" without guilt and "yes" without resistance and resentment. The newfound clarity on your values and self-respect make it easier to communicate and maintain boundaries in ways that feel authentic and sustainable. It's these clear boundaries that will leave you with more energy for what truly matters.

What to Be Prepared For: Strengthening your boundaries can be uncomfortable—both for you and those around you. Not everyone will celebrate your boundaries, especially if they've benefited from your lack of them. Some resistance is inevitable, both from others and your own internalized guilt. Stay rooted in your values, knowing that setting boundaries is an act of self-respect, not selfishness. It will be 100% uncomfortable at first. Over time, though, setting and maintaining boundaries becomes more and more natural as your brain learns to feel safe enough to communicate them with more confidence and less fear of what others may think.

8. Noticing Realigned Relationships

What to Get Excited About: As you transform, your relationships will naturally shift and recalibrate. Some connections will deepen as people resonate with your newfound clarity and confidence, while others may gently fade, making room for those who align with your values and energy. You'll see forgiveness as an act that allows you to move forward, rather than waiting on someone or something else to change. You'll likely find yourself surrounded by those who support, uplift, and genuinely see you, where you cultivate relationships built on mutual respect, trust, and shared growth. Imagine being surrounded by people who see and appreciate you for who you truly are, creating a support system that feels like home. This is one of the most rewarding aspects of rediscovery—a network of relationships that bring joy, inspiration, and peace into your life.

What to Be Prepared For: This realignment isn't always seamless. Not all relationships will withstand the changes you're undergoing, and this can be bittersweet. Some people may struggle to understand or accept the "new" you, especially if they benefited from your previous patterns of people-pleasing or self-sacrifice. You may experience grief or loneliness as certain relationships shift or end, and you're still "finding your people". Not everyone will come along for the ride of this next chapter. This is normal and necessary. Remember that losing old relationships doesn't mean you're doing something wrong; it means you're making space for new connections that truly serve your growth. Give yourself grace during this transitional phase, trusting that the relationships meant for you will deepen, and the ones that aren't will make way for better, more supportive ones.

9. Allowing Yourself to Embrace Vulnerability

What to Get Excited About: When you allow yourself to be vulnerable, you unlock a new level of emotional strength and authenticity. Vulnerability isn't about weakness—it's about courageously showing up as you are, flaws and all. Vulnerability opens the door to deeper connections and empowers you to express your thoughts, feelings, and desires, without fear of rejection or judgment. Instead of hiding behind a facade, you embrace who you are, allowing others to see you in your entirety. This openness creates trust within relationships and helps you grow a stronger bond with yourself. Over time, vulnerability becomes a superpower, helping you navigate challenges with emotional honesty and live in alignment with your values so that you can create space where growth flourishes.

What to Be Prepared For: Vulnerability isn't easy. It can feel terrifying at first, especially if you're used to masking and keeping emotions locked away to maintain control and avoid judgment. Embracing vulnerability means allowing yourself to experience a wide range of emotions and facing aspects of yourself that you may have avoided. As you let your guard down, there may be moments where you question if exposing your true self is safe or even worth it. Some people may respond with discomfort or misunderstanding, and this can sting. However, these moments are opportunities to discern who deserves a place in your life. Remember, vulnerability isn't about sharing with everyone; it's about sharing with the right people. This willingness to be open with yourself and others is where true growth happens—it's the gateway to embracing your most authentic self and fostering the relationships that truly matter.

10. Recognizing and Embracing Your "Enough-ness"

What to Get Excited About: As you strip away layers of societal expectations, outdated beliefs, and survival-mode behaviors, you'll begin to rediscover a version of yourself that's worthy and whole simply because you exist. Recognizing your "enough-ness" brings a profound sense of peace and self-acceptance. It's the equivalent of finally exhaling after holding your breath for years. You'll begin to see that you are inherently worthy, just as you are, without needing to prove or earn validation. This inner knowing is freeing; it lifts the weight of needing to "keep up" and lets you set boundaries, prioritize self-care, and live in alignment with your values. You start recognizing your achievements and your strengths without feeling the need to be or do more. You'll start to measure yourself *not* by others' standards, but by your own standards and values, and the resulting fulfillment and joy you feel in your own life. This is freedom in its purest form—a life where you stop chasing and start living.

What to Be Prepared For: Recognizing your enough-ness may require confronting long-held beliefs that tell you otherwise. In a world that promotes constant self-improvement, you may wrestle with internalized beliefs that you need to achieve more to be worthy. At first, it may feel radical—even uncomfortable—to step off the hamster wheel of "more." You might wrestle with thoughts like, "*Am I doing enough?*" or "*Am I good enough?*" Be patient as you challenge old conditioning, and remind yourself that growth is about returning to your true self, not endlessly striving to "fix" yourself. The journey to enough-ness involves unlearning, and unlearning takes time. Trust the process and celebrate the small moments when you notice yourself honoring your needs and showing up as you are. These are milestones on the path to full self-acceptance and living in alignment with your essence.

You may be noticing a pretty common theme in all of these areas– **be gentle with yourself**. Treat yourself like 5-year-old you needed to be treated. You are now the new parent to the version of you that's been too scared to show up. Know that it's only natural for your brain to resist change, regardless of how much it may benefit you, but you are also the only person that knows what it will take for you to feel safe enough to carve a new path forward.

Lastly, remember that the end of one journey is just the beginning of the next. There is no true "finish line", where you can finally say "I'm healed." Learning about yourself is a life-long process, and just as you think you've finally "made it," there will always be new lessons to learn. This is where life gets really exciting. Every time you become more aware of yourself and your relationship to the world, there's more to learn and implement as you level up. Life is a never-ending game, and the rules tend to all be made up, but each time you make it to a new level, you become even better and better at playing it. You're not just the player. You're the programmer.

And with that awareness alone, you're ready to start your own metamorphosis, enter into your chrysalis era, emerge from your internal cocoon, and spread those butterfly wings and **fly.**

Oh and one more thing! My favorite thing ever about butterflies— they rest in the rain, because it damages their wings.

Rest when the storms come...because once it's passed, you'll be dry and ready to fly.

For more support options, including an online community space, visit
www.themillennialreset.com

www.ingramcontent.com/pod-product-compliance
Lightning Source LLC
Chambersburg PA
CBHW070455100426
42743CB00010B/1625